SO-ABR-596

HOW TO DEAL

IN ANTIQUES

By

Donald Cowie

Founder of International Antiques Yearbook

and

John Mebane

Editor of The Antiques Journal

Babka Publishing Co.
Dubuque, Iowa 52001

Library of Congress Catalogue Card Number 72-83651

Copyright by Donald Cowie & John Mebane

All Rights Reserved

Printed in the United States of America

First Printing May 1972
Second Printing Sept. 1972
Third Printing Dec. 1972
Fourth Printing Oct. 1973

Dedicated to the much-maligned dealer,
without whom so much beauty would be dust.

Antique Shops come in all sizes and shapes

Contents

Preface 6

Chapter I: THE PERSONAL SIDE 7

Chapter II: THE SHOP 13

Chapter III: BUYING 21

Chapter IV: SELLING 29

Chapter V: ADVERTISING—RESTORING 38

Chapter VI: WHOLESALE AND EXPORT 46

Chapter VII: THE SPECIALIST 52

Chapter VIII: INCOME TAXES, ETC. 61

Chapter IX: ANTIQUES DEALERS 67

Chapter X: A POCKET HISTORY OF FURNITURE.. 73

Chapter XI: A FINAL WORD 89

Selected Bibliography 94

Appendix 108

Preface

This book has been written to meet a swiftly growing demand. Many persons have asked for it. The objective is to help them. They will not, of course, expect to learn how to become antiques dealers in one lesson. They will regard this book as it is intended to be—not the last word but primarily a guide.

The material in it is based on the experience of many people and on the unique knowledge of antiques shops that has been acquired by its authors, one of whom has been a successful dealer.

The proliferation of antiques shops that has occurred in recent years is indicative of a coming boom in the broad field of antiques and other collectible objects. You may think the boom is already in progress, and indeed it appears to be—but its peak lies ahead.

Certainly more persons are collecting *something* today than ever in history. There are several reasons for this. In the first place, we have more leisure time than our parents and grandparents had and therefore need a pleasant hobby. In the second place, antiques have proved themselves as a profitable form of investment; and we have found that a sound investment is an essential in an era in which inflation seems to have become a fact of economic life. Moreover, in an age in which the future is in doubt, there is a reawakening of interest in the past, and all that was part and parcel of it from its social customs to its decorative adjuncts.

Today the antiques dealer may not be as essential as the grocer, the baker, and the light fixture maker, but he is on the way.

The authors are grateful to many of the leading members of the antiques trade who have assisted them with facts and advice.

Chapter I

The Personal Side

The most important factor in antiques dealing is the antiques dealer. Therefore the first matter for the aspirant to decide is whether he suits the job and the job suits him. It is possible in politics and some of the other minor arts to get by with a minimum of aptitude but in antiques certain definite personal qualities must exist or there is sure failure.

The primary quality is a flair for buying and selling. Did the tyro delight as a child in taking his mother's old clothes down the road and selling them for pocket money? Did he do a thriving trade in jack knives or match book covers at school? Then he possesses the first and most important attribute of the successful antiques dealer. If, on the other hand, he has curled away from the sordid traffic of the market place, dislikes taking a profit, has a constitutional inability to haggle, then he will be no good.

The second personal requisite is taste, or a reliable aesthetic sense. Antiques are the tangible best of the past preserved. They cannot be identified by an eye which prefers chromium to silver. The person who likes to buy and sell but lacks taste will be as great a failure in an antiques shop as he would be a success on the stock exchange. One way to determine whether taste is possessed is to visit alternately outstanding galleries of furniture and ceramics, and a succession of parlors in suburbia, then compare reactions. Be honest. If the galleries and museums are boring, then do not venture into dealing in antiques, at least not yet. Taste can develop.

The third requirement is knowledge. It is possible to be a foreign minister without a knowledge of French or Spanish, but the dealer who knows nothing of antiques is quickly nudged into bankruptcy by those who do. He buys articles that are not genuine at too great a price and sells articles that are genuine at too low a price.

Knowledge can be acquired. It is possible to study constantly antiques and books and articles about them until learning, like taste, suddenly clicks into place. The beginner would be greatly helped by a few years in the employ of a good firm.

It emerges, therefore, that three personal qualities should be possessed by the prospective antiques dealer: an aptitude for buying and selling, good taste, and a knowledge of antiques, of which the last two can be patiently acquired. The first must be innate and is accordingly the most important.

The reader of this book is strongly advised to examine himself severely in terms of the above observations and not to open an antiques shop if he or she fails to pass the test. He might know more about ceramics than Geoffrey Godden or Richard Carter Barret, but he will be unable to sell them profitably if he is the sort of person who must bestow all his worldly riches on the first beggar he meets. He may be a genius of finance but a poor antiques dealer if Queen Anne furniture gives him the jitters.

Undoubtedly the ideal antiques dealer is like the hero of that excellent novel for would-be antiques dealers—*Quality Chase*—whose hero is a lad brought up by a marine store dealer at the wheelbarrow's end, then inured at the bench to carpentry and carving and polishing, afterwards, driven by a desire for knowledge to educate himself in antiques at all costs. But few children in these days want to be antiques dealers. Most of our readers will be adults, since taste comes late.

Assured of your aptitudes, then, you can proceed to consider further factors making for success that are personal in origin.

It is best to have some money. Capital is always available to the impudent, but it is necessary to possess a steady set of nerves if a business is to be run with creditors at the door. And it will be found that persons with the qualities for successful antiques dealing, such as artists, are apt to be jangled by worry. The nature of the business is such that demands are made on the emotions. There will be a week of bad business, then a good sale. There will be difficult customers, exciting customers, the discovery that an expensive mistake has been made in a purchase, and there will be a constant attack on the emotions by the sheer pleasure that comes from handling beautiful or otherwise fascinating pieces of the past. Some of the most successful and sober antiques dealers in the United States are still creatures liable to alternating moods of exhilaration and depression, the inevitable concomitants of any pursuit connected simultaneously with the arts and with money-making.

So it is preferable that the beginner should be relieved from undue preoccupation with the whereabouts of his next penny, since so many dealers have attempted to start with next to nothing.

The amount of capital required to open an antiques shop will vary widely, according to geographical location and the type of business established. In the United States, business expenses, ranging from rent to advertising and printing, are almost invariably higher in the larger cities than in the smaller communities. In the smaller towns rents in "prestige" or high traffic count areas are usually considerably higher than in less desirable locations. It would be misleading, therefore, to attempt to give hard-and-fast figures. The best way to estimate the amount of capital required is to work out as accurate an estimate as possible of rental and allied charges to be paid over a period of say three months, and add to this the preliminary cost of stock. If the dealer desires to live on his shop premises, he may also want to take his personal living costs into consideration, and there are many dealers who do combine their business and living quarters. He should have in hand not only the total sum estimated for three months of expenses *but also an additional sum* that will be available for buying at sales and privately during the preliminary period.

Solely for the sake of an elementary example, here is a case in which the beginner starts in a town of approximately 75,000 population in a desirable location but not in the heart of his downtown business district:

3 months' rent	$ 375.00
Utilities, advertising & miscellaneous labor	150.00
Stock to start	2,000.00
Printing	50.00
	$2,575.00

Those are the bare essentials. If a telephone is desired—and it will be most advantageous—one must include an additional sum, often a $100.00 deposit, plus about $11.00 a month (or $33.00 for the three-month period) for limited service facilities.

Moreover, if a business license is required, as it frequently is either by the county or the city, the cost of this will range from $10.00 to $100.00 or more on an annual basis.

But on the *bare bones* basis outlined above, the beginner should possess at least $3,575.00, the additional $1,000.00 being his standby for unforeseen expenses which so often rear their venomous heads at the least opportune times. Remember, moreover, that in this specimen example we are treating of a small, obscure, almost ideally insignificant business; and we are still ignoring the day-by-day phenomenal increases in ordinary costs, which are the plague of this present inflationary period in history. A signboard with the word *Antiques* in white lettering on a black ground which costs $35.00 today may cost $45.00 by the time these words are published.

The three-month cost estimate cited above may range to as much as $800.00—$900.00 more in such a metropolitan area as Minneapolis or Atlanta or decrease by about $100.00—$200.00 in a rural area in which rent and labor in particular are cheaper.

It is a good rule, however, to capitalize your outgoings over a period of three months and have enough in the bank to meet them. Your true economics expert would recommend, of course, a much longer period and consequently a far greater sum, but if such a doctrine of perfection were applied, then it would be possible to establish a new antiques business only on a syndicate basis.

Whether to buy an existing business or to create a new one; the questions of locality; type of stock; private dealing, and extent of stock will be discussed in the next chapter. The subjects have been introduced here only in relation to their bearing on that personal element of capital required.

The figures given above should be multiplied proportionately to the size of business contemplated. A well-known shop with stock in a good country town is offered for sale at $20,000. In addition to that initial outlay, the purchaser would be required to have in hand sufficient capital to tide him over at least three months of settling down. A well-stocked shop in an excellent location in a city of nearly 100,000 population is offered at $50,000, including the building. An empty suitable house on a main road in a smaller community is offered for $16,000. There are many different ways of starting an antiques business, and these will, as we said, be discussed in the next chapter.

We advise, however, that at least $3,575.00 of capital be available for the start of the most modest kind of antiques shop.

These comments do not apply to the start of dealing in antiques as such. You can buy and sell a piece here and there in your spare time at home and gradually amass capital. Some of the most famous of modern dealers are still private dealers even at the height of their fame and fortune, without shop, warehouse, or trade name. This type of dealing also will be discussed in greater detail later on but does not properly concern the question of how much capital is required for an antiques shop.

A further personal attribute that we would strongly recommend from considerable experience with and knowledge of antiques shops is a possession of a partner of the opposite sex—and this is meant in no jocular sense. The man who sets up as an antiques dealer without either a wife or a mother, or maybe a sister, is at a tremendous disadvantage. He will probably be unable to afford a paid assistant at first. As a bachelor or orphan without relations (spare the tear!) he will have to leave his shop locked up every time he goes out to inspect an article for sale or to deliver a piece, or attend a sale. The average dealer who expects to make a go of his shop is likely to have to travel around the countryside with some regularity to buy goods and to be away from his shop an average of half of each week. It will be increasingly to his advantage to be away, as will be seen in the chapter on *Buying*.

Given as partner a wife similarly interested in antiques, the dealer has someone to look after the shop while he is away. He has, moreover, a feminine influence upon his shop and stock-in-trade which is very noticeable when lacking. Women are very successful in the antiques trade. We know one old lady who is regarded as the shrewdest and wealthiest dealer in her area. We know a large business managed most efficiently by a girl. Many of the best antique shops, particularly in rural areas, are operated by husband and wife in equal or almost equal partnership. A woman is often the shrewder buyer, though the man may be a better salesman. Trade buyers prefer, it is admitted, to deal with "the boss."

We deliberately used the term "partner of the opposite sex" when introducing this matter, because what applies to a man who starts an antiques shop also applies to a woman, who is at a similar disadvantage without a man, if only in the background. There is a clear distinction here between partnership as such and what we are suggesting. Proper partnership, as between two men or two women, or between a man and a woman, is not necessarily recommended in the initial stages of a business. An experienced dealer has actually said to us: "Never take a partner." We are referring rather to the advisability of the tyro having someone in the background who can attend to his business in his absence and supply that touch of the opposite sex without which a shop can be too masculine or too feminine in atmosphere.

Other personal qualities are age, aptitudes in various subjects or professions that bear on antiques, and the actual disposition of the would-be dealer.

Age, it has been proved often enough, is in itself unimportant. Not far from New York is a foremost specialist dealer who completed nearly a lifetime's successful career as an engineer before he retired a few years ago, found the weight of taxation and rising living costs heavy, and decided to dispose of his private collection of antiques in a small shop. This man is now recognized as a leading expert on his subject and would be making a second fortune if the times and the Bureau of Internal Revenue allowed him. At the other end of the scale is a young man in Atlanta, Georgia, running a big business against strong competition in one of the city's best shopping areas at an age when many of his contemporaries are inefficiently running unimportant errands.

The very young, however, are not advised to start an antiques shop unless with the advantage of family experience and/or capital behind them; while older people with sufficient funds to support them independently are advised to think hard before taking on the worries of an entirely new business in their remaining years. A sound general rule might be not to embark upon full-time dealing in antiques before 25 or after 65.

Previous commercial experience of any kind is most valuable, and the older person who wishes to become an antiques dealer may sometimes have personal advantages such as aptitudes derived from study or a former business or profession. It is most useful to possess skill in woodworking and a liking for evening hours at the bench. Architects have often made highly successful antiques dealers, because they have been trained to recognize historic and stylistic periods and have the jargon of the classical orders and decorations at their finger tips. Artists usually know something about pictures and can be apt at restoring. Engineers with their mechanical knowledge have sometimes drifted into extremely successful horology. Auctioneers and estate agents can turn to dealing in antiques with an intimate knowledge of values. Former military and even police officers, of whom there are a number in the trade today, bring the advantage of courage in dealing with difficult situations and charm in dealing with customers.

This brings us to the personal quality of disposition (in the sense of the impression presented to the world by a man or woman). But this is actually the first and most important quality in antiques dealing and was dealt with when we discussed the preeminent requisite of an aptiude for buying and selling.

No one can buy or sell successfully unless he is capable of hard decision on the one hand and soft persuasiveness on the other. It is no use opening an antiques shop if you are all hard or all soft. The most successful dealers invariably possess great charm of disposition as well as a hard decisiveness of manner when buying as against selling.

Lastly, as a famous Scottish dealer reminds us—*hard work*. He writes:

"This may frequently mean giving up prearranged pleasures and forgetting holidays, or even time in general. I do not think there is anything more important in the building up of an antique business than application to it, irrespective of time or personal inconvenience. As witness the fact, that in my earlier days I had a large placard in my window as follows: 'Hours of Business—7 a.m. to 7 p.m.' Then in large red lettering below 'Other hours by Appointment.' "

Chapter II

The Shop

There are several kinds of antiques business—the small shop, the large shop, the department of a store, the private house open to the public, and that of the individual who operates privately without showroom.

The small shop is best located for the beginner in an inexpensive quarter of a good area for antiques. That almost certainly means outside the city limits and even the suburbs of such devastatingly crowded metropolitan areas as New York City, Chicago, Philadelphia, Boston and other overgrown and overcrowded municipalities. There are excellent areas for antiques in these burgeoning cities, but these are expensive and constitute the highly-competitive stamping-ground for the most experienced dealers in the trade, who have graduated there after a long struggle upwards from the quieter regions outside.

We write in terms of the average man. There are cases where beginners have sailed straightway into New York's Third Avenue-lower Broadway-University Place areas and have succeeded But the rents for the more suitable buildings therein would eat up the average newcomers' capital in short order, and the competition of more experienced men would break him in any case.

The net profit and sum of human contentment of many a diminutive antiques dealer in smaller communities and the country are often much more considerable than those of not a few well-known traders in the New York City area bounded by Broadway and Fifth Avenue and 11th and 14th Streets.

Be wary, moreover, of the suburbs of these teeming giants, no matter how rich or reputedly lavish with socially-aspiring residents who *should* buy antiques. The suburbs are essentially dormitories, places in which people sleep and occasionally stir a spade in a Lilliputian garden. The antiques-minded inhabitants of these suburbs prefer to buy their treasures in the city shops or in quaint country towns on week-end voyages of exploration, or holidays.

It is not sufficient, however, merely to pick a smaller town or a country area at random. There is an extraordinary difference between the prosperity of antiques dealers in these lesser areas that cannot always be attributed to obvious causes. The shops in one industrial town, for example, may prosper while those in a nearby college community may languish. Some of the South's thriving cities with a good many bookshops and a considerable number of inhabitants who buy antiques possess scarcely a dealer of importance, while almost decaying towns miles from anywhere sometimes boast several flourishing establishments: within a few years the position may be reversed.

Choose a town that already has one or two prosperous dealers: that is RULE ONE. In other trades competition may be dangerous to the beginner; in antiques it is very valuable. If there are two or more shops in a town it will be worth visiting by the week-ender, the tourist, and the trade buyer. Browsers can spend a morning there and a long drive will not be wasted. So individual is this business that no two shops are apt to be in the least alike. One will tend to have furniture and the other bric-à-brac. One will stock first-class and the other second-class pieces. One will feature imported antiques and the other American primitives.

In New Orleans there are famous antiques districts, but why do we also visit little Murfreesboro, Tennessee? Because there are dozen or more antiques shops there, all different and most of them reasonably prosperous.

Then, antiques dealers, like farmers, can be very cooperative, and, especially to beginners, most helpful. Provided you do not tread directly on the big man's toes, say by concentrating on his own specialty of Chinese porcelain, he will likely go out of his way to assist you in your struggle upwards, send you customers, give you advice, and even buy from you.

Choose, then, a town where there are prosperous dealers already, preferably in a part of the country that you know well. An antiques business could be conducted successfully on the summit of one of the Great Smoky Mountains by the right man or ruined in Boston by the wrong one. Then take note of some of the observations we can make about the respective merits of various parts of the country.

New England is an excellent region for antiques and so many that are native to the region still abound that competition for them has not yet quite reached the cut-throat stage. Auctions at which good buys may be obtained dot the countryside. Not only are many New England farmhouses still treasure troves of early country pieces, but New England estates have even attracted dealers from England, who purchase fine antiques that originally were made in their own country for shipment back to their native land.

In addition, the states of Vermont, Massachusetts, New Hampshire, and Maine boast many outstanding museums and village restoration that preserve the region's own antiquities and serve as a stimulus to interest among the populace.

On the other hand, the South, by and large, remains a region in which the majority of those who buy collectible objects seek such things as country furniture and "primitives." Fine French and English furniture often go begging at auction sales, and, except for a handful of dedicated collectors, the average purchaser eschews fine porcelains and art glass. One reason for this is that there seems to be a greater lack of knowledge in the South than in other regions about the better and costlier antiques. Another is a fear of reproductions.

This is not to say that there are no fine antiques in the South. There are, many preserved in white-columned antebellum homes, either still owned by descendants of the original builders, or acquired, restored, and furnished with taste by newcomers, a fairly large percentage of whom have emigrated southward from other areas of the country. But in most such cases, only a well-equipped burglar could pry these possessions loose from their owners, at least until they fall upon difficult times.

Certain of the more cosmopolitan cities of the South, however, are becoming good areas for the sale of antiques. New Orleans is famous for its long row of shops along Magazine and Royale Streets and in other areas. Miami, Florida, with its influx of winter visitors from the North, is an excellent area, especially for dealers who display their wares at the periodic shows. In Atlanta, which today has become perhaps the most cosmopolitan city in the South by virtue of its swift growth as a distribution and regional sales center for national business organizations, there are more than two score of shops within the city limits and many more within the sprawling metropolitan area. The majority, however, are relatively small and specialize in inexpensive collectibles. The bulk of antiques selling is done in this area by auction houses and fairly large wholesalers. Three auction houses handle desirable lines of good antiques; others sell primarily second-hand merchandise, primitives, reproductions, and trifles. Many of the higher-priced antiques are purchased by decorators with commissions from wealthy families. Despite some dedicated efforts, Atlanta has not yet come of age as a city of culture and a widespread appreciation of the arts, though it may be on its way.

In addition to Miami, several other areas in phenomenally-growing Florida offer good possibilities for the would-be antiques dealer. Both Jacksonville, on the Atlantic coast, and Tampa are growing swiftly and are good possibilities for dealers who can cater to both the local and the tourist trade. Much smaller St. Augustine, one of the South's historic areas, boasts the Municipal Lightner Exposition, founded by the late O. C. Lightner, who also founded and published *Hobbies* magazine. The museum is now owned by the City of St. Augustine. There are a number of antiques shops, chiefly small, in the city that sell largely to visitors.

Although the states of South Carolina and Mississippi provide a variety of attractions for tourists, there are few major antiques shops in either (with the exception of the city of Charleston in the former), and it appears doubtful that local populations at present would support many of them. North Carolina, among the South's most progressive states, is beginning to do a thriving business in antiques, and large wholesalers have recently established businesses there. A similar situation prevails in Virginia, which, with a lion's share of families of old aristocratic stock, affords some excellent possibilities for additional antiques dealers, particularly in such areas as Richmond, Norfolk, and Portsmouth.

Perhaps the Western states offer the would-be dealer the greatest possibilities of all, particularly in the realm of collectible objects associated with the settling of the West and with the romance and glamor of the late eighteenth and the nineteenth centuries. In California, the second largest state in the union, interest in Western collectibles is reported at a peak with a booming trade being done in such metropolitan centers as Los Angeles and San Francisco. The new dealer would probably thrive best outside of one of these sprawling cities rather than within the overcrowded municipal limits.

Good locations also exist in the suburban areas surrounding such other cities as Portland, Oregon; Denver, Colorado; Salt Lake City, Utah; and Dallas and Houston, Texas. Certain areas of the West are still sparsely settled by comparison with New England and the East. The potential antiques dealer who carries the right stock may earn a modest livelihood in the area of such cities as Phoenix, Arizona; Sante Fe, New Mexico; Witchita, Kansas; Omaha, Nebraska, and Des Moines, Iowa.

Although bottle and flask collecting are currently popular throughout the United States, the peak of interest is in the West, with bottle clubs and associations and bottle shows proliferating like rabbits. Several dealers who handle bottles and bottle books exclusively are presently doing well in small communities in the West, though a large part of their trade is carried on by mail.

In other areas of the country, good potentialities exist close to such large cities as Chicago, Illinois; Milwaukee, Wisconsin; the Minneapolis-St. Paul twin cities in Minnesota; St. Louis, Missouri; Louisville, Kentucky, and Knoxville, Tennessee.

There is a smattering of shops in the following areas, which are not yet overcrowded with them, however, and may provide a challenge for the enterprising and imaginative dealer: Little

Rock, Arkansas; Birmingham, Alabama; Indianapolis and Fort
Wayne, Indiana; Detroit and Grand Rapids, Michigan; Akron,
Toledo, Cincinnati, and Cleveland, Ohio, and Scranton, Pennsyl-
vania.

Considerable wealth, along with a fairly large number of shops,
is concentrated in cities such as Pittsburgh and Philadelphia,
Pennsylvania; Baltimore, Maryland; and Washington, D.C.-Alex-
andria, Virginia.

Pennsylvania has long been prime "antiques country." Some
areas of the state are overcrowded with shops, but dealers from
throughout the country continue to trek into Lancaster County
and others, seeking sources of stock, and a number of wholesalers
do a brisk business during most of the year.

By and large, coastal resort areas are good during the tourist
seasons but relatively poor during the remainder of the year.
Even so, dealers willing to work at their job (and those who are
not should never enter the field in the first place) may be able
to earn a year-around livelihood with well-planned shops in
some of these areas, particularly those with still-growing populations. Among these, to name a few, are St. Petersburg, Florida;
Savannah, Georgia; Wilmington, Delaware; half a dozen medium-
sized communities in New England; Long Beach and San Diego,
California, and Biloxi, Mississippi.

Other locations with fine possibilities for the imaginative and
knowledeable dealer include those with historic associations. In a
number of these venturous promoters have re-created historic
spots, buildings, or even entire villages. Some such ventures
have been undertaken with the unselfish and certainly commend-
able motive of helping to preserve the American past. Outstanding among these are Old Sturbridge Village, Sturbridge, Massachusetts, and the Shelburne Museum, Shelburne Vermont, to mention
only a couple.

Throughout the United States, knowledgeable and hard-work-
ing dealers have proved adequately that a metropolitan location
is by no means essential for a successful shop. An impressive
list can be compiled of unusually successful establishments in
small and even relatively little known communities. These include
towns with whose names you may not be familiar, such as
Arlington, Vermont; Prides Crossing, Massachusetts; Woodbury,
Deep River, and Old Lyme, Connecticut; Lambertville, New Jersey; Exton and Downington, Pennsylvania; Middleburg, Virginia;
Winnetka, Illinois; Hopkinton, New Hampshire; and Shelbyville,
Kentucky. In some of these relatively small communities not one
but two or three prosperous shops exist.

Here are some general rules to bear in mind when seeking a
location:

RULE ONE: A town that already has one or two prosperous
shops.

RULE TWO: A main route.

RULE THREE: A place of historic or scenic interest which can be made to cater to visitors.

RULE FOUR: A small shop, rented as inexpensively as possible, with good space for display and storage, and with living accommodations combined.

It is better to rent a shop than to purchase one unless you have considerable money and/or simply want to invest in property, because otherwise if all your capital will be sunk in a purchase, you will have none for buying stock.

Try to avoid a short-term lease, or you are likely to be faced before long with the problem of either paying higher rent or finding new premises—and this is a problem that could rear its menacing head just as you have established yourself.

The shape and overall floor-space of the interior are important. Remember that you will not be selling shoes or bakery products but sideboards, pictures, Peach Blow vases, or perhaps dry sinks and an occasional wicker perambulator. It is necessary to visualize such stock in the small proportions of the shop offered to you and decide whether you will be able to store and display your goods effectively there. Alas! some beginners have taken shops without first learning whether the doorways are wide enough to admit antique furniture. Be certain, too, that the premises are not damp, or infested by dry-rot, termites, or wood borers. If there is any doubt at all, it may pay to have a careful investigation made by an independent expert.

Wide window space is ideal for the display of antiques, but this may be denied the frugal beginner. The ideal can be attained later, with success. But the window should preferably be at least of plate glass descending nearly to ground level. Be cautious about shops with steps leading to door or window. These are a menace to elderly customers and to carriers of fragile articles, and accidents could lead to law suits.

Regard your potential neighbors with interest if not suspicion. Should the man on the right be a mortician and a lady on the left a somewhat faded variety of the genus beautician, you will obviously not be in company conducive to the kind of customers you want. Places of public entertainment, bargain stores, garages are not advisable for neighbors. Those who buy antiques like gracious thoroughfares, pleasant surroundings—or a series of junk shops punctuated by a prize.

At the rear of the shop it is advisable to have storage space and a place that can be converted into a workshop with bench and light and heating. A side or rear entrance is more than useful.

We advised that living accommodations on the premises be obtained. The beginner or his wife might not like to live over a shop, but can always remember that scores of their social betters are paying high premiums at the moment for apartments converted from such accommodations over the shops. (Besides, if any inhibitions are felt at this stage about anything connected with shops or shopkeeping, it is best for the sensitive soul to retreat at once and finally from the whole business.)

Some of your best customers will arrive on a Sunday afternoon or at half-past eight on a Monday evening. If yours is a lock-up shop with a nebulous re-direction on the door to your inferior place of suburban residence some miles of streets away, you will probably lose those best customers. If you live on the premises, you can open to good fortune at any hour and work amid your stock at any spare moment. In your own absence on buying trips it also will be easier for your wife to attend to the shop.

There are some communities in some states that still do not permit business to be transacted as usual on Sundays, but these are declining in numbers, and a growing proportion of antiques shops now open after church hours on Sunday afternoons, which are still the only afternoons that many working men have for leisure, their Saturdays being occupied with the serious business of attending sports events.

We are led from this to a brief consideration of the private house kind of antiques shop that is becoming increasingly popular. It is quite a good idea provided the house is not *too* private. In many communities zoning regulations prohibit the opening of business establishments in predominantly residential areas or in other areas not specifically zoned "commercial." So make certain that you check into zoning matters before you plunge into a lease on a house, no matter how attractive otherwise it is.

If properly zoned, a restored cottage or bungalow on a main road, a Victorian house on a well-traveled street in town, or even an abandoned church parsonage on an easily-accessible thoroughfare are sufficiently in keeping with your calling to pass. We mention the parsonage primarily because one of the coauthors of this book did indeed open an antique shop successfully in such an abode, while an enterprising retailer opened a carpet sales establishment in the erstwhile church adjacent. Needless to say, this area had been rezoned "commercial." We believe indeed that the successful antiques business of the future will increasingly occupy premises of this kind. The customer must often overcome considerable hesitation before he enters a very small shop that looks more like a home than a business to look around. He can, however, enter the hospitably open door of an interesting old Victorian house and wander from room to room without undue self-consciousness.

Yet the beginner is not advised to saddle himself with the great expense of purchasing, decorating, fitting-out and furnishing such a house. A cottage is the most he may aspire to in average circumstances, and cottages are being utilized with increasing frequency and success for small businesses.

If your financial means are limited or public premises are not immediately available, you can still attend sales in your spare time and buy antiques to be sold at a small profit either through advertisements in newspapers or the various collector periodicals or through the trade. With the mounting scarcity of salable antiques, many established dealers buy from individuals (to whom they often refer as "pickers") who are lucky enough to obtain good buys at public or private sales.

This is probably the best way of determining whether you have the qualities essential for successful dealing in antiques, and such an experiment could well decide your future. When at sales (as dealt with more fully in the next chapter) buy only, and cheaply, what you feel to be genuine and good and capable of yielding you sufficient profit to pay your expenses and net profit—or buy at a higher price what you think is really good *in the absence of big dealers*. Advertise your acquisition after cleaning, minor restoration, and polishing.

By selling to the trade is meant making your acquisitions available to those retail and wholesale antiques dealers who travel the country regularly in search of stock. The names of such dealers may be obtained from antiques magazines and periodicals or even your city telephone directory, and you will soon have your regular trade friends and callers.

The private dabbler—indeed the beginner with his shop and the finest established firm—cannot have better advice than to be content with small profits. Thus he will be blessed with quick returns and, soon, with a good reputation. But this is a matter for the later chapter on "Selling."

If you do dabble privately before deciding to enter upon full-time antiques selling as a career, you would be well advised to subscribe to some of the collector periodicals in which appear not only advertisements of articles for sale but, in most cases, ments of articles wanted. Among these are:

The Antique Trader Weekly, Antiques, The Antiques Journal, Antique Monthly, Antiques News, Collectors News, Collector's Weekly, Collector's World, Hobbies, The Mid-America Reporter, National Antiques Review, Relics, Spinning Wheel, Tri-State Trader, and *The Collectibles.*

The largest of these is *The Antique Trader* with a circulation of more than 85,000 copies throughout the United States and publishing frequently as many as 100 pages per issue. Addresses of the various periodicals will be found in the Appendix to this book.

Chapter III

Buying

We discuss buying before selling, as it is the more important. In no trade is it so important as in antiques. This is because (1) a dealer stands or falls on the genuineness and right price of his goods, and (2) you cannot rely, as the shoe merchant, upon fresh deliveries of replacement stock from factories each week.

The buyer must be able to decide at a glance whether the piece is right or wrong and what it is worth. Old furniture rarely bears formal marks of origin as such. Sometimes an 18th century invoice may be stuck yellowed on the back by a former noble owner or by a recent ignoble cheat. The finest French furniture bears the signature of the *ébéniste*. But the tables, chairs and cabinets offered to the beginner at local sales will yield him no definite clue of origin, nor will much of the pottery and porcelain available. China marks might be defined as trade marks of the early factories which are to be found in many reference books but seldom on china. Only silver carries its certain label.

There are many indications of age and period which can be learned and are helpful. Certain kinds of mahogany were not used after a certain date. There was a time when cow-glue ceased to be used and when the flat-pointed screw was superseded by the sharp point. In every kind of antique there are many subtle aspects of design, which help to mark the approximate age. Knowledge of these aspects can be acquired by handling as many antiques as possible and by talking with experts and, of course, reading. What is needed is knowledge that is concerned largely with chronology or the time factor. Learn to think almost woodenly in terms of dates and periods. Afterwards you can blossom out into appreciation proper.

Appreciation—the discernment of the true aesthetic value in a piece—must take into consideration perfection of workmanship and the sum-total beauty of the article's appearance, which will be found to depend upon niceness of proportions, color, patination, and excellence of decoration.

But commercial value is affected by more factors than these, by more than the exact age and beauty of an object. The buyer must know that at the present time, if not yesterday or tomorrow, great oak buffets, no matter how lovely or right, are not in profitable public demand; that exquisite bronzes, on the other hand, are suddenly back in fashion; that good Federal Period furniture will continue to be wanted although second-rate pieces of that period may become a drug on the market; that elaborately-decorated silver requires overmuch cleaning for the modern home; and many, many similar facts of the moment.

There is the question of degree of restoration. "Furnishing antiques" are those bought and sold for modern household use and decoration." "Collectors' pieces," by contrast, are those acquired for inclusion in a public or private museum of antiques. The buyer must be able to tell into which category an article falls, and this depends not just on authenticity, beauty, and fashion, but upon the degree to which it has been touched, or restored. The Queen Anne bureau with brasses of another period loses value as a collector's piece, although it may sell well enough as a furnishing antique—provided that the point is made clear to the purchaser. The old coffee pot lacking a cover may sell in the shop to ordinary customers as a flower container but will not interest a collector.

All these points about a piece discerned dustily among the piled offerings of a salesroom preview must be judged by the buyer quickly and unerringly, or he is lost. There is rarely time or occasion for crawling under tables for prolonged sessions of probing with penknives or scrutinizing with magnifying glasses. It is equally rare that a potential buyer will have the opportunity to take the Meissen or the Chelsea figure home and boil it for breaks before purchasing.

It should be emphasized at this point, however, that antiques cannot be bought successfully according to formula. The piece of porcelain may lack decoration or mark or shape comparable with any already known, but the expert feels that it is the work of Thomas Tucker or of Smith, Fife & Company, and probably he is right. He goes upon the characteristic cold feel of the early American hard paste, and he marks its strangely pleasing shape. An instinct has been developed at the back of the brain in coordinating knowledge read and experience acquired, based upon an initial flair.

Unquestionably that flair must be present in the beginner if he is to succeed. Its presence can be tested only by such an experiment as visiting a friend's house or shop and, from the depths of ignorance, attempting to assess the periods, authenticity, and value of the pieces there. A patient friend may or may not be disposed to cooperate in such an experiment.

It has been demonstrated that buying is important because antiques take some buying. The second reason for the importance of this major aspect of dealing in antiques, namely the unique difficulty of replacing antiques stock, also requires some explanation.

The general public seldom appreciates the fact that genuine antiques are no longer produced. Whereas salesmen call daily upon other shop owners with samples and catalogues from which they may order for immediate delivery just as much of a given commodity as they require, the antiques dealer can invoke no such systematic source of supply. Given a godsent customer who buys half his stock in an afternoon, the dealer may be very happy—until the dreadful thought interposes that he must do something quickly to replace that stock or his turnover and thus his income will diminish by half in the coming week. That is why wealthy dealers are sometimes as sorry to sell as they are glad to buy.

There are four main sources for buying:
1. Auction sales.
2. Other antiques shops.
3. Wholesalers, including exporters.
4. The public privately.

The beginner may find by investigation that certain firms of autioneers locally or in nearby towns have a better class of trade than others. Possibly all auctions will be worth a cursory visit or inspection, but the best to attend seriously will soon be found. In addition, the dealer will find it advantageous to study all local newspapers and those of adjacent communities within striking distance so as to be apprised sufficiently in advance of casual sales at private residences. Then he will obtain catalogues or lists when these are available and view the objects to be sold in advance of their actual sale. This will be his serious hour, the time for deciding whether or not to bid at the sale and how far to bid. The catalogue should be marked, in a simple code, with the maximum prices he is prepared to bid.

It cannot be emphasized too strongly that the beginner should get into the habit promptly of regarding his sale bidding as a cold-blooded progression towards a ceiling price—and no farther. Too many dealers, even old and experienced hands, allow themselves to be carried away by a kind of gambling, competitive emotion, which only plays into the hands of the sellers and lands the emotional bidder in financial difficulties. Possibly it is true that at certain times like the present a dealer cannot bid too highly for a rare collectors' piece, but the beginner—if he is wise— will not be concerned with such. He will be wise to stop bidding if several prominent dealers from other areas are present. He is small fry and must be content with small prizes from unimportant sales until such time as his knowledge and capital are sufficient. This may require great patience, but there is an old Dutch proverb that says, quite wisely, we think, that an ounce of patience is worth a pound of brains. And meanwhile, he can watch and learn.

There is, of course, a strictly illegal institution known as "the ring," which manifests itself chiefly in areas where several large dealers congregate. If the beginner were invited to join, he should consult his conscience, or he may be swayed by his temperament. There are those who prefer the hard way of complete independence, and there are those who prefer the warmth and material advantages of society. It depends upon whether you are the type of man who becomes a Mason or Rotarian, or whether you are the type of man who does not. With age most of us appreciate the more what a formidable task is undertaken by the Lone Ranger and how foolish is the beginner who eschews the hand of fellowship.

Perhaps you should take into consideration the excuse that exists for any "rings" that do operate at antiques auctions: this is the presence on equal terms at such sales of both dealers and the general public, which would ordinarily place the dealers at the disadvantage since *they* have to buy and sell again for their livelihood.

Probably the best advice that can be given the reader throughout this book is to watch and follow in the footsteps of established dealers until such a time as he is competent to walk surely for himself; and that will be quite a considerable time.

The most important auction sales of antiques, apart from those held occasionally at large private houses, are held in New York City by Sotheby Parke—Bernet and a handful of other auction dealers and in a relatively few other large cities. Some of these should be attended, if possible, if only to learn. Not long ago it was possible for even the beginner to buy a few furnishing antiques at these auctions when prices sometimes fell below the provincial for the second-rate. Within the past few years, however, the competition for virtually all antiques, even the second-rate ones, at these prime auctions has been so great that prices have been forced up in many instances to well above what the beginner can or should afford. There have been some indications recently of a tempering of this bidding fever, and perhaps the occasion may again arise when the neophyte can purchase a few items at these great sales.

An almost indispensable weapon in buying is a motor vehicle, preferably a pickup truck, small van, or station wagon, or at the very least, an old car with wide doors and a substantial top. The beginning dealer may not be able to afford commercial transportation on goods bought in New York or Boston but could easily take home some pieces in his own vehicle.

A vehicle also is essential for the second source of antiques buying—from other antiques shops. Though it may not be generally realized, it will soon be discovered by the beginner that the roads and highways of every state know the constant traffic of dealers visiting each other's shops to buy. Undoubtedly the novice will be bewildered at first to understand who makes the profit and how in these considerable interchanges of the same goods, although he may learn in due course when he is himself the "last buyer" of an expensive piece which "sticks;" but the fact is that each dealer has his own clientele and local preferences. Oak may be selling well in Dubuque, Iowa, so the dealer there visits shops in localities in which it is not selling so well and buys cheaply. Then each local dealer acts in a sense as the buying agent for others. He buys at the local sales which only he can profitably attend not only those goods he can sell in his own shop but also goods that he know other dealers will be glad to take when they call on him. This trafficking among shops is extremely widespread and is becoming heavier annually.

There is customarily a trade discount, which ranges normally from 10 to 30 per cent below prices at which the goods are sold to the general public, but do not take this for granted when buying in an unfamiliar antiques shop. Some dealers prefer to allow their goods to fetch the best prices they can; they will quote an absurdly high price even to a fellow dealer and be prepared to come down as much as 50 per cent. Yet others stand hard by one price both for the public and the trade. These, it should go without saying, are scarcely good marks for the trader, unless the prices quoted are indeed low.

The average antiques dealer finds its profitable to travel fairly extensively, sometimes several hundred miles a month, to buy stock. It is of interest, too, that in this country, a far greater percentage of dealers buy from other dealers than from auctions. One reason is that dealers dislike buying in competition with their retail customers, some of whom make astute mental notes of what the dealers purchase and at what price and then check the markup that these dealers place on their goods in their shops. On the other hand, there have been evolving of late a series of auctions held for the trade only, and these do afford dealers protection against both the competition and the snooping of their customers.

The dealer who begins on a small scale, especially if he lacks competent help in his shop, may well find at first that he will do better to avoid regular trips and, apart from buying at sales, obtain his goods privately from *wholesale dealers.*

There may still be some who insist that no wholesale and retail exist in the antiques trade, and this might have once been so but is no longer the case. Every area of this country has dealers who specialize in buying for the trade, even though the majority of them are concentrated in New York City. Many of these do not admit the general public at all. There are even some who sell rather extensively on the installment plan to small dealers. Many wholesalers advertise in *The Antiques Dealer, The Antique Trader Weekly* and other antiques magazines. The advantage to the beginner of utilizing such wholesale services is that he can thereby concentrate on establishing his business from the selling end. It is important in the beginning that he should pay his rent and salary by sales in his shop to local people and visitors. It is regrettable if he must leave this to an untutored assistant or even an untutored wife while he is away. But he can attend the local sales, replenish stock otherwise from wholesale sources, and encourage local people to sell him goods privately.

Buying privately is very important. You do not have to pay auctioneers' or wholesalers' profits, and you have no traveling expenses. Often those dear elderly ladies who bring you their treasures with so much pretense of selling them solely to make space for better pieces are themselves potential customers or will introduce their wealthier friends to you.

Methods of obtaining this type of business include posting notices in your window that you buy antiques, constantly reminding your customers that you buy as well as sell, and advertisements in local newspapers.

There are a few pitfalls in attempting to buy privately. A few unscrupulous dealers will rig so-called "private collections" and attempt to sell them to you through a stooge. And there are some "dealers" who rent homes in residential areas, fill them with collectible and a good many non-collectible objects, frequently at higher prices than these objects fetch at retail in the shops, and then advertise "private house sales." Such houses are rented from a month to a year, and the way to spot these rigged "private sales" is to watch for newspaper advertisements in which the same street location appears week after week.

A legal point worth remembering as a buyer is that people often offer antiques and other valuable items for sale when they possess no title to the property in question—when they have stolen the goods, or are part owners only (as in the case of some heirlooms). If there is any doubt in your mind as to the status of the seller, you should require him to sign a receipt that contains the words "I hereby warrant the above articles to be my own personal property, over which I have full and unconditional right of disposal."

Antiques buying is different again from that in other trades by virtue of its predominantly cash basis. Credit may be offered by a few wholesalers, but the beginner must be prepared to maintain a good balance in his bank account and carry his check book everywhere for daily use. The goods he buys at sales must be paid for at once; and it is always best to offer and pay cash to other dealers and to private sellers. This is expected in fact. A dealer's credit is built on years of cash payments ,until one day it is so good that he is readily invited by other dealers to participate in large syndicate purchases of important pieces without immediate cash payment.

This aspect of the trade is good for the beginner, because it saves him from overspending, the temptation of which is constantly present and sometimes overwhelming. Antiques dealers present a singularly honorable front to the outside world as compared with traders in some other businesses. If they have sometimes in the past earned a reputation for over-astuteness, this has not resulted from any defect of record in meeting obligations. The dealer who breaks the unwritten law of pay-as-you-go is soon ostracized if not literally drummed out of business.

While on the subject of buying, it may have been noticed that throughout we have taken it for granted that the beginner starts an entirely new business with an empty shop, or with stock taken only from his personal collection. This is because we have been unable to recommend the purchase of an antiques business as a going concern. Much money can be sunk in this manner. It is perhaps all very well for an experienced man to buy an existing business, taking stock and "goodwill" at valuation. But the beginner is best advised to start from scratch in a new shop.

The "going" concern has the disadvantage in this particular trade of antiques in that it often ceases to "go" on the retirement or death of the proprietor. As emphasized in the opening chapter few trades are really so personal. The successful dealer's good will is almost wholly bound up in his own presence and personality. His customers come to him, not his shop. His knowledge of both antiques and customers cannot be replaced. Who buys the "goodwill" of an antiques business only too often buys a chimera.

As for the stock involved in such a purchase, it can so easily be the residue, the dregs even, of what was once an excellent stock before the proprietor began to sell off the best pieces. By purchasing stock with an existing business, you buy dross with the gold and perhaps will also have another man's mistakes to add to your own. Also another man's character. You will want your business to represent your own personality and ideas. So buy gradually and carefully for yourself and through the channels we have recommended, starting with a clean sheet.

A well-known American dealer comments on this: "It isn't essential that you slavishly follow the fashion in buying. If you buy what *you* like, your stock will reflect *your* taste and personality. The stock that is different or that reflects the individuality of its proprietor will attract its own customers."

A Scottish expert made a wise observation: "Experience in buying and selling must come the hard way. Book knowledge is useful and visits to museums are to be advised, but it is only by buying one's mistakes that one can ever appreciate values and be successful in the long run. It is therefore to be recommended that one start very modestly so that the mistakes which one must make may not be too costly.

"Furthermore, it is unfortunate that the examples which one sees in museums, or which are referred to in the normal reference books, are, generally speaking, items that are not found by the small antiques dealer. In other words, he is much more likely to find Sheraton tea caddies or Pembroke tables than fine Chippendale commodes or Queen Anne kneehole desks.

"I can clearly remember the story of one man who started in the antiques business with a small fortune but no knowledge. By buying his mistakes in the course of ten years, he was left without his fortune, but had accumulated some useful knowledge. Eventually the position was reversed, and his knowledge helped him regain what he had lost.

"I think another point which should be brought up is the advisability of *avoiding* bargains. So often one is tempted by the price at which one can buy an item, and not by its quality. These 'bargains' invariably become shopwatchers, whereas a good item which one likes and pays a fair price for will sell a hundred times over.

"Another point that might be mentioned is that while in London most dealers become specialists, in the provinces goods of every antique description must be handled. London has its china merchants and its silver merchants and its furniture merchants, who deal exclusively in these particular classes; but if a shop is to be started in the provinces, one must cater, or try to cater, to everybody.

"Still another very important point, and this I think is really the dividing line between a successful and the unsuccessful antiques dealer, is the correct assessment of the selling value of an item irrespective of its cost. An item must be sold at the selling value and on its own merits rather than by rule of thumb where the same ratio of profits is applied to everything. It is the *replacement* value which one must consider when selling an item, and *not the actual cost*.

"I do not think it is quite true to say that all good antiques [in England] eventually reach London. The bulk of them may be located in the metropolis, or may find their way there, but certainly not all of them."

This expert's advice may be translated into American geographical terms. New York, Philadelphia and other major cities have their specialists in one category of antiques or another, but those who locate in the smaller towns and in suburban areas should be prepared to cater to as many different types of buyers as possible.

All good antiques by no means gravitate to New York, although the bulk of them may eventually find their way there. Some of the finest come from private owners in states from Maine to Florida and from California to Texas.

Chapter IV

Selling

It will be assumed, as already has been noted, that the beginner is to concentrate at the outset at least on building up a good shop business. He must take care to make his shop attractive.

There are fashions in antiques shops as in all else. Some years ago the public undoubtedly preferred the old curiosity or semi-junk shop atmosphere. Even the wealthy collector felt himself at home among cobwebs and clumsily piled articles ranging from good porcelain to second-hand clothes. He believed that he was most likely to discover a bargain therein. And he liked his antiques dealer to be an old man with creaking joints or at least a humorous character somewhat in the Gallagher and Shean tradition.

That fashion has passed. Some such shops remain, it is true, but they are no longer representative of this business as a whole. Wealthy buyers are catered to by antiques establishments which, indeed, often go too far in the sumptuous direction, consisting in one or two extreme cases of little more than a heavily-piled carpet and a single treasure dominating a vast gallery like the lone milliner's model in a Park Avenue hat shop. Ordinary people are frightened by overdone ostentation of this kind, but like tidiness and cleanliness, brightness and an appearance of something at least akin to prosperity.

Let us try to give a picture of the type of antiques shop that appears to be most successful and popular at the present time. It is tastefully decorated, either in black and white, or black and gold, or pure white, or some pleasing pastel shade, preferably with a period-style window. The sign "Antiques," with whatever accompaniment, must be conspicuous, preferably both on a hanging board and on the front of the establishment. It is a great advantage for other signs to be erected at intervals of several hundred yards or even miles down the road, directing the motorist to the shop, in the case of suburban locations and those in which such signs are not prohibited.

Preferably the shop has an unusual or a quaint name. We think of such successful, proprietary designations of existing shops as

29

(do not exactly copy them) "The Mad Hunter," "The Pavilion House," "Sleepy Hollow Shop," "Whimsey Antiques," "Treasures Unlimited," "The Red Brick House," "Gooseneck Antiques," "Half-House Antiques."

Some elegant brass and copper hung outside is an advantage for the beginner as it will attract the eye of the passing motorist. The trade in more sophisticated areas has tended to become ashamed of brass and copper, but it remains justly popular with the mass of people interested in antiques and is very useful in attracting customers in those large untutored sections of the community from which the antiques buyers of the present are being drawn in this age of increasing equality. We may buy Ming horses today but never forget that we were first attracted into an antique shop by a warming-pan or a gooseneck kettle. Brass and copper are all right so long as they are genuine. The metals have been debased in our time by reproductions at home and abroad, which, if stocked, should be kept carefully in an isolated part of the shop and sold as such.

Within the window of a popular shop is a selection of attractive articles, polished and preferably with some price and interesting descriptive labels, at least on the cheaper pieces. Keep the window scrupulously clean. The middle of the window is the best selling position, then the right-hand side of the window. Always turn the handles of the jugs to the right.

The question of whether or not to "touch"—that is, partly to restore and clean and polish—has been fervently debated in the trade in recent years, but results in shops show that the "brighter and better antiques" school has definitely won the day. Some old dealers maintain, as all once held, that collectors prefer their antiques "untouched." If the library table has ink stains on the mahogany, do not remove them. Leave the dust in the crevices of the porcelain figures. Let the pewter attain its dull patina and the silver remain tarnished. Allow the missing section of marquetry to remain missing. And go easy with the duster, even, lest a precious flake of gilt be flicked from the freize of the fauteuil.

All this at the time might have been demonstrated as foolish, in that antiques are preserved by loving care and not by lazy neglect. The best pieces of the past are those kept long in some loving house and daily polished by prim though tender hands. How shocking, on the contrary, to encounter an historic relic in the mud!

A sense of proportion is required. To French-polish an antique by modern shortcut methods is criminal, as it is to regild a mirror frame, touch up a piece of pottery with color, or replace the worm-eaten slat of a chair with a piece of new timber. But it will be found that the public which buys in ordinary antiques shops today appreciates clean, bright, and reasonably sound pieces. Moreover, antiques kept in good condition make an excellent colorful display. We remember how we were so used to seeing dirty Staffordshire figures that when we encountered an array of them under electric light in a shop after they had been carefully washed by a dealer we momentarily believed they were porcelain.

The stock of the popular shop today, then, is clean. We must add that it usually has price labels.

Again, the old school would have protested. Some of the finest old dealers today still refuse to affix prices, partly from pride, partly from their method of doing business, which is to vary the price, as doctors used to do, according to the overcoat or the haggling ability of the customer. But as recorders of what is happening, and as honest friends to the beginner, we must state that the tendency is all the other way. Prices are clearly marked, retail first and perhaps code wholesale and code cost below. Thus the public is entitled to browse and make its calculations as to whether or not it can afford to buy. In this way we meet the prejudice in many persons' minds that the goods that have no price on them are so dear that the shopkeeper is ashamed to make the open statement (which he will later confide to you in a whisper, lest the shock do you some physical harm). And we indicate that we do not profiteer but have one clear price for all—and, at the same time, a clear basis for percentage reduction to the trade.

Indeed, the National Association of Dealers in Antiques, Inc., a major organization for the trade, includes among its planks of ethics the clear marking of prices on pieces offered for sale by its member shops.

And what of those prices? In the successful, popular shop of our study they are never excessive, always fair, and on a level with the majority of those charged by dealers elsewhere in the geographical area.

There are two ways of selling antiques. One is to enjoy a large turnover at the lowest possible profits. The other is to affix an absurdly high price to a piece and sit down and wait, usually in a dimly-lit shop, perhaps for a year until an unwary customer comes along and gives you as much profit in an afternoon as the other man makes in months of honest dealing. Judging, however, from the brighter mood, smarter appearance and greater popularity of the first man, we advise the beginner to follow in his footsteps. He will enjoy a clear conscience when successful. He will not by his actions be doing grave harm to the trade which is his only hope and livelihood. And we believe that he will really prosper more than the profiteer.

What is a fair profit? The answer could be that it is a profit that enables the shopkeeper to pay average expenses and live at an average standard. One dealer informs us that he put on 25 per cent gross, then another 25 per cent for himself. But there is much more to it than that. Should a dealer pick up a genuine piece of Tucker and Hemphill porcelain at a sale for a few dollars, he is entitled to sell it at a rate of several hundred per cent profit. On the other hand, the beginner will need to stock certain articles on which the profit will be very low. These will be items that are quite popular and that many customers expect to find in a shop. Possibly the best way to fix profit is to sell always at the "list" price of an article—the price customarily charged by other dealers—and to remember this in the salesroom before you buy so that you do not buy unless you can obtain the article at a price that will enable you to sell at the "list" price and still make enough profit to pay your expenses.

There *is* a list price for most fine antiques. Whether in Bangor, Maine, Portsmouth, Virginia, Dubuque, Iowa, or Tampa, Florida, it will be found that a corner cupboard of average quality costs roughly the same price. A Benjamin Randolph chair, a Simon Willard Banjo clock, a porringer by Paul Revere, Sr., a Phoebe lamp—they have at all places approximately the same price among alert, honest dealers. The exception proves this rule, because absurd prices charged by a profiteering dealer are so obvious to the experienced buyer.

Moreover, the appearance in recent years of price guides for antiques compiled by experts in the field have had an equalizing influence on the prices of even those more recent collectible objects whose values earlier had varied from locality to locality. The most current of these is *The Antique Trader Price Guide to Antiques and Collectors' Items,* issued quarterly.

Perhaps the best advice that can be given the beginning dealer is that he visit as many other good shops as possible and note carefully the prices obtaining there and that he read as fully and as carefully as possible the price quotations in one or more of the various collector periodicals published in this country.

It can now be seen why we may have appeared in the preceding chapter to have overstressed the importance of buying. Unless the dealer buys at the right price, he cannot sell at the right price and at the same time make his legitimate profit. The vital rule, then, is to buy only at prices which enable you to make your profit and not overcharge the public and not to permit yourself to be swayed by a sentimental affection for an object you intend to buy and sell.

Unfortunately the tendency of this leveling age is for the public to want more cheap and less expensive antiques. At the same time, small families, diminutive modern houses and apartments, and lack of household labor underline the demand for minature pieces and those that involve a minimum of upkeep and attention.

The beginner is consequently advised to stock in his shop a considerable number of pleasant mementoes of the past that can be priced at not more than $25 and if possible not more than $15. He will find that three-fourths of his casual customers will be unready to spend more than $25. Similarly, he will try to stock primarily small furniture, plain silver, and avoid elaborate rococo design.

Also, be careful at first of oak. Few persons of taste collect much oak at the moment, despite the recent vogue for round "golden oak" dining tables and other dining room adjuncts of this wood. If you do buy oak of older periods with a view to satisfying a few good customers, you may well burn your fingers, since no type of antique furniture can and has been more easily and prolifically faked. Again, however, much depends on the locality of the shop. Good oak will sell very well at the right place, so keep an ear to the ground.

What the general public responds to most quickly in the small shop today includes small pieces of atractive furniture in mahagony and walnut, colorful porcelain and pottery, Colonial and early 19th century silver, convex and oval mirrors, antique jewelry and even pieces from the Victorian era, and, invariably, curious small articles of local interest that can be retained as mementoes. The furnishing aspect is becoming increasingly important as the wealthy class which heretofore provided the great collectors finds itself strangled by taxation and increasing financial problems. The real collectors in your area are apt to be members of the relatively impecunious masses, interested in souvenir spoons, inexpensive pattern glass, coins, pottery and china of the more accessible varieties, such as Rookwood and Dedham, and early bottles, bells, and mechanical banks.

It is unhappily true that most small antiques dealers experience a considerable demand for reproduction articles. The definite law to be laid down here is that you cannot mix it. Many try, but only to find the character of their business subtly changing. They no longer have an antiques but a second-hand or new furniture shop. Buyers of taste tend to shun such establishments. Accordingly, the very strict rule should be enforced that reproductions when stocked be carefully segregated from the genuine stock and should not in any case exceed 25 per cent of that stock.

The demand will be experienced chiefly for small mahagony pieces of furniture, dining and miscellaneous tables, and bureaus. Try to avoid reproduction china, glass, metalwork and mirrors. if only because their very appearance cheapens the appearance of the shop itself. With the current tremendous influx of reproductions of glass and metal in particular, this will not be too easy to do unless the dealer himself learns to distinguish between the originals and the modern copies, some produced in original molds and with the use of the early tools. This ability to distinguish will come with experience and can be hastened by the reading of authoritative books on antiques.

There is, on the other hand, no objection to stocking a modest proportion of appurtenances to antique furnishing schemes, such as door furniture, a few hand-loom fabrics, and lamps made from old materials— always provided that the display of these is not allowed to dominate the shop. The best furniture polishers and metal cleaners, plate-hangers and the like may be discreetly displayed on a side-table, as may reference books on antiques.

Should the dealer be interested in interior decoration, he may arrange with a local firm of decorators to carry out schemes for his customers to his design at an agreed percentage of profits. Many dealers also give decorator-customers the same discount from list prices that they give other dealers. This decorating aspect of antiques retailing can become important in the operation of the business.

It should be remembered that when a customer is sold two or three antiques he can sometimes be persuaded to plunge farther and find that he also requires not only appurtenances to these but, further, a suitable background in his home, from decorations to curtains. We know one dealer who, from initially selling a customer a piece of pewter, was eventually responsible for remodeling the facade of his house.

All of which brings us to the culminating factor of actual salesmanship, about which so many volumes have been written. We certainly do not propose here to teach the art of selling, which is wholly personal and not to be acquired from a short lesson.

There are two personal methods of salesmanship: leaving the customer to buy without undue persuasion except perhaps for a quiet word here and there, and persuading the customer to buy at all costs. We have watched both methods in action, deploring, on the one hand, the lack of enterprise of the seemingly tongue-tied if not actually rude dealer, and regretting, on the other hand, the effect of force on a customer who might decide never to enter the shop again after being so over-persuaded

The best method is a combination of both. The customer should be sold the article in which he is interested at all costs— but quietly and insidiously rather than with a display of "hot" salesmanship with its verbal pyrotechnics more suitable to the fairgrounds or the political arena than the pleasant atmosphere of an antiques shop.

It is deadly wrong to assume that antiques sell themselves, and it is wholly right to remember that you are in the shop for one purpose only—to sell antiques. Never be the least ashamed of this role. And do not fear that the customer will hate you forever if you sell him something which he is not absolutely convinced he wants. It is a psychological fact that we are nearly always pleased with purchases once we have made them—*because we have made them.* It is a poor thing but mine own.

This is always qualified by the proviso that the article sold is genuine and fairly priced.

As in all other human activities, truth is best in dealing in antiques. The most successful dealers take care to point out to the customer all the obvious faults in an article before metaphorically taking off their coats and persuading the customer to buy at all costs. And it should be emphasized to the customer that should the article subsequently prove to be a reproduction, a fake or otherwise not in accord with the description, then it will be taken back and the money paid for it refunded in full. The best dealers give such a guarantee on their invoices or receipts, which also contain a description of the goods and some reference to approximate date (i.e., "18th century" or "circa 1850" or "Federal period"). If there is any doubt about the period, append the word "probably."

The antiques trade has not always and does not even now invariably enjoy the best of public reputations. Many ignorant people still think that dealers are necessarily scoundrels or con men. It will be found that all too many customers enter the fray aggressively and seem to be constantly doubting and suspecting. Dealers should make every effort to break down this prejudice by scrupulously fair behavior and by employing devices such as those suggested above to disarm criticism. Most persons engaged in this business today are wholeheartedly behind this effort, and a sound, almost professional status is slowly being acquired. After all, physicians who were quacks and sawbones not many decades ago are regarded today with something akin to respect and we have heard good words said for lawyers as a result of scrupulous adherence to a code of professional ethics.

Charm of manner goes a long way in selling antiques. The acquisition of objects of beauty literally refines the mind and emotions, and your solid antiques buyer responds with fellow feeling to well-chosen words, pleasantly spoken, and to courtesy which is not too subservient. Friendships are made over antiques, but nice people do not make friends with boors.

Knowledge provides another community of interest and weapon in salesmanship. This should be displayed unostentatiously and cautiously, but firmly enough when based on a sure foundation. There was a time when dealers could get by with little knowledge but a very keen commercial sense. This time has passed. Antiques buyers want to be told today where a piece came from, its approximate age, and what are its special points. You will find that questions as to origin and age will be asked you with an almost amazing consistency by your customers, young and old, short and tall, knowledgeable and ignorant. And you should be prepared to answer. Often this may require homework in the form of research after you have acquired a piece, but the knowledge gained will usually be worth the effort.

Finally—the question of payment. In the preceding chapter it was emphasized that dealers usually pay or have to pay cash for the articles they buy at sales or privately for stock. On the other hand, and most unfortunately, they often have to extend credit to their customers. This is quite safe enough where good local customers are concerned, even though a bit aggravating in the financial sense. It will now be obvious why we suggested earlier that the beginning dealer have on hand capital to last for at least three months without taking into consideration shop receipts for that period. Again, many dealers engage in the custom of accepting checks even from strangers and allow them to take away articles with no more payment that a promise to pay and a name and address.

A common way of avoiding financial embarrassment when credit is sought by a buyer unknown to you is to suggest that the piece be retained in the shop and marked "sold," to be delivered later when the customer has made full payment.

Many shops today utilize such a plan for instalment buying, holding the article purchased until the final payment has been made. When selling on the instalment plan, however, it is wise to stipulate a date for the full amount to be paid.

The widespread use today of a variety of bank and other credit cards does much to help guarantee payment to the seller, provided the rules of the issuing institution are rigidly followed. It would be wise for the dealer to determine what type of credit card or cards are most widely used in his own community and then to contract with the issuing agency to accept its cards. Most such bank agencies will provide an imprinting machine for a small annual rental. You must remember, however, that such banks and other credit agencies charge the seller an amount generally ranging from 2 to 3 per cent of the retail cost of the article sold in exchange for guaranteeing and making payment. Payment in such cases is made direct by the guaranteeing bank or other agency to the seller, and almost invariably quite promptly.

Some dealers contract with two or more credit agencies, but it will be found that in the majority of the smaller communities only one type of credit card is generally used. Agencies providing such credit will furnish sellers with placards to be placed in the shop, informing customers that its cards are accepted. Although acceptance of credit cards does impose a small financial "penalty" on dealers, many sales may result from their use that would not otherwise be made.

There is also the matter of delivery of merchandise that cannot easily be removed by the purchaser in the latter's car. The dealer should make such deliveries free up to a certain distance from the shop, and consequently the cost of delivery should be included in the price before it is fixed. Many dealers stipulate that the customer must arrange to pay for the cost of delivery beyond a specified radius of the shop. The distance for free delivery may range up to 10, 25 or 50 miles. For delivery beyond the maximum distance, the customer should pay the actual cost.

When out-of-town customers make purchases and ask that articles be sent to them via parcel post, express, or freight, they should pay the charges for such delivery. Such shipments can be made on a collect-on-delivery basis for the actual transportation cost if it is impossible, as it often will be, to determine actual charges beforehand.

Selling to the trade is much easier in all these respects. The trade buyer requires no buttering up and is quick to make decisions. He pays at once and almost always takes the piece with him.

Chapter V

Advertising-Restoring

Two distinct arts, those of advertising and of restoring, must now be considered as adjuncts of the successful running of an antiques business.

It has been found by a study of successful shops and of the media for antiques advertising that in this business as in most others the most successful firms are those which publicize themselves properly. There are some that do not advertise and still appear successful, but these are very rare exceptions to the rule. When a visit is paid to the shops whose names have been made familiar by advertising, these are invariably found to be the best, while the majority of nonadvertisers are by comparison usually dull, unreliable, and over-expensive.

The dealer with the courage and enterprise to advertise widely is necessarily a keen man, and a keen man sells the right goods at the right price because he is keen.

There is a novel entitled *Quality Chase* in which one will encounter Joseph Chamberlain's exhortation to a young antiques dealer bewailing a lack of customers and asking for help. There are your customers passing outside, says Chamberlain. Go out and get them! The moral is that a dealer must not only buy right and have an attractive shop and sell right, but he must inveigle the customers inside. If possible, he must attract them from afar. The most effective way of doing this is by advertisement in certain media.

The beginner should include in his expenses for each year an allocation for publicity purposes, say $350 to $500, and should be most careful at first not to dissipate this on unproductive local advertising. He should take an occasional small ad in his best local newspaper, but he should turn a persistently deaf ear to salesmen for school, church, and local magazines, for menus, calendars and tourist guides (unless such guides are well-known and established). Do not be afraid of offending the captain of the baseball team, the school superintendent or the minister in this respect. It is rare that such individuals buy antiques, and the circulation of their periodicals is nearly always small and their readers few. With your limited allocation, you cannot afford to spend wrongly. Experiment cautiously, if you like, and test the results. Ask customers if they came in response to an advertisement and record in a book or on a chart comparative results from the different media.

If you expect to sell over any wide area, the first and most important media for your advertising messages are your own trade publications: *The Antique Trader Weekly, The Antiques Journal, Hobbies, Collectors News, The National Antiques Review, Spinning Wheel,* and *Collector's World,* among a few others. These have fairly wide and proved circulations among your potential customers, and their readers are persons genuinely interested in antiques. If your plans embrace prospective large sales to dealers, you also may wish to consider *The Antiques Dealer,* whose circulation is among the trade exclusively. And if you handle certain rare and expensive pieces, you will want to consider the magazine *Antiques.* No one uninterested in antiques would read any of these publications. And you will find that nearly all antiques dealers of any importance, and, in addition, large numbers of smaller dealers do in fact advertise in one or more of these periodicals.

Some of the magazines will be used more than others by the trade and for different purposes. Most of the periodicals listed above are issued monthly except for *The Antique Trader,* which now appears weekly in tabloid newspaper format and claims to be the widest used of any periodical in this field in the United States, and one or two others.

Antiques is especially effective for the selling of major and important pieces, although its advertising rates are substantially above those of the other publications listed. Rates of most of the others, in fact, are less than those for want ads in many of the larger daily newspapers.

The Babka Publishing Company, which publishes *The Antique Trader* and *The Antiques Journal,* also issues an annual *Directory of Antique Dealers,* in which advertising is sold at a low cost and which is an effective medium for advertising your shop, its location and what type stock you offer for sale.

Some beginners think that in advertising it is a case of "all or nothing." They think they must place a full-page advertisement or none at all.

This rule undoubtedly does apply to dentifrices and detergents but definitely not to antiques. You would never get your money back if from a very small shop in Slippery Rock you took full pages in the major periodicals each week. How could you? Advertising expenditures must be related to potential turnover. Even if those advertisements brought hundreds of tourists a week to your small shop in Slippery Rock, you would hardly be able to recoup your expenses, not having the facilities or the stock.

Therefore, take initials announcements in your trade publications, increasing the size as your turnover and facilities increase. Should your purchase an important piece, it will pay to take larger space in the trade publications with an illustration to accompany it.

Good photography is important and may present some difficulty unless you boast photography among your own accomplishments. Local photographers accustomed to immortalizing wedding groups rarely know how to photograph glass or metals. On the other hand, some newspaper photographers with whom photography is both a profession and a hobby, can do an excellent job for you. Many of these are available in their time off from their regular jobs.

What you will need is a sharp black-and-white glossy print in which the background is either a plain cloth or can be brushed out and in which details, such as those of carving, reeding, pattern, marks and highlights, are perfectly reproduced. The print must also be of a size capable of being reduced or enlarged proportionately to the size of the projected illustration in the advertisement. Do not send color photographs to most of the publications listed, because photographs in color nearly always reproduce much darker than they should in a black-and-white engraving. They may look good to you but they do not look good to the engraving camera. Of course, a few periodicals do publish advertising in color, and the illustrations for these should be color transparencies.

One major dealer does advise us that he does not believe in over-elaborate professional photography. He thinks that psychologically it is better to buy and sell from a poorer photograph, since, in such a case, the antique when it arrives does not disappoint the purchaser. Also the amateurish picture looks "honest." Still, the viewer is not able to judge much of quality by a blurred or badly-cropped photo.

A photographer will charge you in most cities anywhere from $5 to $25 for a 5x7 or 8x10 print. Most periodicals that have their printing done by typesetting will charge you for making an engraving at approximately their own cost, usually $5.00 to $10.00 depending on the size of the engraving. At least one periodical that uses offset printing, however, has announced that it will use cuts for advertisers without any additional charge for their reproduction. The engravings become the property of the magazine publishing them after they are used. Many dealers take their own photographs at far less cost.

Before leaving the subject of photography, we recommend that the dealer preserve in careful index form photographs of all the interested pieces that pass through his hands. Much selling is done by photograph. It will be found that, in response to advertisements, inquiries will be received from other parts of the country, and frequently from other parts of the world, and photographs enclosed along with responses to such inquiries often effect sales.

There are a few general magazines whose readers respond to advertisements of antiques for sale. Among these we can recommend *Yankee,* which began as a New England regional magazine but now has readers throughout the country, and a few of the home-and-gardening magazines, such as *American Home.*

When advertising, do not confine the announcement to the name and address of your shop and such a general account as "Furniture, Porcelain and Glass." Say something intriguing about the character or whereabouts of your shop, such as "The smallest house in Tuscaloosa," or "Located in Underground Atlanta," and specify the particular point that is most likely to persuade potential customers to write or visit you: "Collectors' Paperweights and Art Glass;" "Specializing in Federal Period Furniture;" "Early Cast Iron Toys and Mechanical Banks;" "Grandfather and Banjo Clocks Always in Stock." You are bound to have or develop some particular specialty, and it has been definitely proved that readers respond to such specialties in advertising, while their minds slide over the smooth, routine surface of a general statement in this as in all forms of artistic expression.

Not only photographs but also drawings are valuable attention-getters; for example, an artist's impression of the outside of your shop, of your unusual signboard, or of a charming antique piece such as an early Sampler or an American Windsor comb-back chair. You can probably find a local artist in your town who will execute such a drawing for you at a cost of about $15 or $20, and you can use this, made into a small line engraving for a few dollars, not only in advertisements but also on letterheads, envelopes and labels. It will help identify you and make you known among the hundreds of others who are in jostling competition with you.

There are, of course, other forms of advertising, although we cannot recommend billboards, which are in bad standing with a growing number of municipalities, or printed circulars (because it is at first so difficult to get the names and addresses of potential buyers and a fortune can be wasted on circularizing the wrong people).

Municipal and regional antiques shows afford dealers an opportunity for a special and important kind of publicity: the opportunity of making widespread contacts with trade buyers and private collectors alike and of publicizing the whereabouts of the shop and its specialties.

These shows have increased in numbers and importance in the past few years, and today it is a remote area indeed which is not reached by one. The majority of these shows are handled by private promoters, but even many of these today are "sponsored" by charitable and other organizations, which receive a part of the proceeds for the promotional help they give and their advance sales of tickets. Some sort of institutional sponsorship also usually results in considerably more publicity about the shows themselves in local news media than would otherwise accrue.

Except for the shows held in the large cities, rental fees for exhibit booths for dealers are not high. They will range generally from $35 to $75 for a show continuing from two to four days. This fee can be recouped with a few good sales at the show, but the value of contacts made and publicity gained during the shows may be greater than that of sales made during the exhibitions. Often initial contacts are made at such shows with individuals who subsequently become permanent customers. Valuable contacts also are made with other dealers to whom you may be able to sell or from whom you may wish to buy. Normally, in fact, there is substantial trade among the dealers themselves immediately prior to the formal opening of these shows to the public.

Many dealers participate in a dozen or more of these shows annually, often traveling considerable distances to reach the good ones. Travel, of course, involves expenses as do meals and lodging away from home; but in most towns and cities one can find suitable motels which charge from $7.50 to $15 a day for rooms, and meals need not be expensive ones. We know promoters of several good shows who provide dealers with free coffee.

Because of the limited space available in the exhibition booths, which will average 10x10 to 10x15 feet in size, the dealer should take along with him for sale a fairly large percentage of higher-priced antiques or two or three good but not oversized pieces of furniture. Many dealers who regularly participate in such shows transport their merchandise in trucks or vans; some rent trucks or vans which are available today in almost every community; and others utilize station wagons. Naturally only a few pieces of furniture—and small pieces at that—can be accomodated in a station wagon. A number of dealers who specialize in displaying furniture at the shows and who have trucks or vans in which to transport it rent one and one-half size booths or two or more booths.

As a general rule, the show promoters provide tables for the exhibits, and the dealers furnish their own shelves and table coverings. The shelving often consists simply of boards, set upon such things as waste baskets and covered with paper or cloth. Individual booth lights also are provided by the dealer, but the promoter makes electrical outlets available to each exhibitor, sometimes without additional charge, sometimes for an added fee.

One is likely to find that the less expensive 19th century collectible objects sell better in the smaller towns than do the earlier and costlier antiques, but this is not invariably the case. For example, shows in some of the smaller resort communities catering to tourists often attract collectors of considerable means who visit these shows in anticipation of bargains and rare finds.

The shows in metropolitan cities such as New York, Detroit, Chicago and others usually involve higher expenses, both for booth rental and for away-from-home living costs, but aggregate sales at these shows usually total rather staggering sums.

In addition to the regular shows, there also are "flea markets" in which some dealers participate. Contacts can be valuable at the better known and larger of these, particularly those held in conjunction with community-wide commemorative events. The majority of flea markets, however, are still held out of doors, and the dealer is therefore subject to the whims of the weather. Consequently, the small dealer is advised not to travel too far from home base for the flea markets.

Dealers who gain a reputation as experts on antiques have additional opportunities for promotional activities in their cities, especially through appearances on local radio and television programs and through occasional newspaper interviews. Although the media are becoming increasingly chary of affording "free publicity" for anyone or anything these days, the majority of radio and television stations and newspapers will mention the name of the shop operated by the individual who makes himself or herself available for an appearance or an interview. Often such publicity is of greater value than paid advertisements.

The ingenious individual will think of other ways to contrive favorable publicity in the media. We know one dealer whose shop was located adjacent to a cemetery and who reported to the newspaper that "ghost birds" had visited the establishment. Time and again, this dealer found feathers on the floor inside the shop when the establishment was opened in the mornings, but never a trace of a live bird. On one morning he found that a large Bristol vase had been knocked off a shelf and smashed to bits on the floor. A newspaper feature writer visited the shop and wrote an intriguing story which was published in the paper. The truth of the matter is that birds had indeed visited the shop, but they were not ghost birds; they were pigeons who were accustomed to roosting atop the chimney and occasionally found their way down it and then back up again.

Sometimes, too, when a dealer acquires a great rarity in an antique or one with which considerable local history is associated, the newspapers will devote a story or the radio and television stations part of a newscast to this. The dealer should make certain, however, not to press his luck too far in this respect, or he will find himself in the category that the media refer to as "publicity hounds" and will be avoided.

There are dealers in some cities who contribute bylined columns on antiques and collecting to their community newspapers. This can be invaluable in publicizing favorably one's name and adding to his stature as an authority. We know one collector who decided to share his knowledge of antiques with others by contributing a weekly column on collecting to his home town newspaper. He eventually wound up by writing half a dozen books as well.

Now for restoring, at the other end of the pole from advertising and publicity, but of equal importance in the success of an antiques business.

It should be stressed at the outset that it is not necessary for the dealer himself to be an expert restorer, whether of furniture, porcelain and pottery, or paintings. It is an advantage, however, if he possesses some skill in elementary cabinetmaking, or possesses or develops quickly a knowledge of staining, polishing, and dealing with the ubiquitous wood borer.

Possibly it may be to the disadvantage of the dealer for him to be an expert cabinet-maker. He could be persuaded into the dubious path of faking or making what amounts to new furniture. If such skills are possessed, they are better practiced as a whole-time job in an establishment properly labeled "Cabinet-Maker."

The ideal is to hire as soon as possible a man who can be trusted not only with minor repair work to stock and to customers' antiques or requirements, but also with heavy work about the shop and storeroom, polishing, delivering and even attending to customers in the proprietor's absence.

In the meanwhile, however, it is advisable to make contact with a reliable local cabinet-maker who will regularly accept your small commissions.

The legitimate boundaries of such work as undertaken by or for the antiques dealer are repairs, replacements of small broken parts, and polishing. If the restoring be carried to such length as the complete replacement of panels and stands, for example, this not only will require skilled craftsmanship but will add to the dealer's difficulties in selling. He should remember this before he buys a fine cabinet minus legs or a gateleg table without a top. If he restores the piece (at some expense), then he must sell at a disadvantage after duly warning the potential customer, or must enter upon the path of perfidy whence, alas, there is rarely any safe return. The cost of restoring is becoming so high in these days of labor and timber shortages that it is seldom worth the effort except in the realm of small, legitimate repairs.

The restoration of pottery and porcelain is a craft that can be acquired by the dexterous dealer, and this is useful if confined to the repairing of pieces for furnishing use or for converting into lamps and similar accessories. But it is a snare and a delusion if practiced by the ordinary man with the idea of restoring to value once-valuable pieces. China must be sold perfect or with the imperfections clearly indicated to the customer. Repairs to deceive the expert and maintain the price are outside the skill and, we trust, the conscience of the amateur.

Most handy persons can learn the craft of restoring paintings. This can be fruitful if practiced, as it should be at first, on what appear to be unimportant old pictures bought cheaply at sales and perhaps as part of a lot. The bright beauty of the pristine paint revealed and revarnished may make of an ugly duckling a highly saleable picture—if not of great artistic value, at least of appeal for furnishing purposes. Once again, the beginner would do well at the outset to make the acquaintance of a picture restorer in his area who will accept his commissions.

One repairing hint is not to permit any of the repairing activities on the premises to be too audible or otherwise evident from the actual shop. Yet some dealers have been known to disregard blatantly this rule. The merry sounds of the saw and plane, the hammer and chisel as well as the smell of paint and glue are not conducive to the peace of mind of the seeker after the genuine, nor are frequent passages through the shop of aproned individuals carrying the frames of chairs in unpolished beechwood or Pilgrim Century joint-stools with unstained pine or maple tops.

The extent of restoration undertaken will be governed largely by the type of the business. If the shop specializes in objects for home decoration, small and local, it will pay the dealer to spend a good deal of time replacing the missing brass handles on a highboy from catalogues obligingly provided by several firms of specialist repute in this line. It will not pay the dealer if his trade is with dedicated collectors. In fact, he will have had no business in the first place to acquire a highboy without handles.

Finally, don't seek to eke out a poor, preliminary income by accepting too many repair jobs from customers. It does not pay today. These jobs rarely yield a satisfactory profit and often relations with the customer are soured by the dealer's inability to have the work done as quickly or cheaply as desired. In addition, a distressing suspicion is apt to enter the mind of the customer who finds that the dealer is so clever at repairing and restoring. The customer might refrain thereafter from purchasing antiques in that shop.

It is best, therefore, to leave restoring on any considerable scale to the restorer proper, and to concentrate as an antiques dealer upon buying and selling genuine antiques.

Chapter VI

Wholesale and Export

The "wholesale" dealer has developed either from private buying and selling as described before in this book, or from a shop that has found its business with fellow dealers to be more profitable than its traffic with the general public.

The individual who starts privately is inclined to become more of a buying agent than a wholesaler pure and simple. Almost every big city has one or more of these, experienced frequenters of the sales rooms and probers of the junk shops, who know that anything they buy at the right price will be taken from them immediately by firms whose acquaintance they have carefully cultivated. There are individuals who travel the country buying chairs alone. Their trucks at the end of the trip are piled high with chairs which are sold in one lot to a large antiques dealer. Nearly every kind of antique has its wholesale hunter or buying agent.

Whereas the buying price is important to successful shop-keeper, it is much more so to the wholesaler, whose profits depend entirely upon the cheapness with which he can buy the articles to be passed on. Therefore such a man must be very expert indeed, and possessed of an innate or painfully acquired commercial sense.

Unfortunately, the inevitable "pickers" and free-lance agents of this profession, possessed less of skill and sense than of eye for the short-term main chance, tend to harm the antiques trade. Should a particular kind of antique become popular or its value increased because of some special circumstance, these pickers emerge and buy all pieces of the kind that they can— good and bad. This elevates the price and soon kills the fashion, leaving legitimate dealers all too often with unsalable stock.

The activity is very much like that of the Stock Exchange. Undoubtedly it can be harmful in such crude manifestations, though equally surely it is necessary and valuable in its higher levels, where a few skilled specialist dealers with considerable capital behind them operate in antiques "futures," fixing a price by the sensitivity of their demand. This is, no doubt, the apex of antiques dealing, since the financier crowns all trades; but we shall not attempt to teach such an elevated art.

The wholesaler who has developed from the shop is usually beyond reproach and often the cream of his profession. He has operated his shop business along the lines suggested in this book of careful buying at low prices and honest selling at no more than legitimate profits. Consequently, other dealers have increasingly found it possible to buy in his shop. He has observed the value of this trade business—a quick turnover for cash without fussing—and also, noting that the times make it increasingly difficult to serve the general public inexpensively, has decided to deal with the trade alone.

Some readers of this book will desire to follow such a course themselves, but they should be certain first that they possess the necessary qualities as outlined above, especially skill at buying and lack of greed in selling. They must be ready to travel and have a wide knowledge of the trade which will be their customer. That will, in its apex, always be the New York trade.

The New York trade is to that of the smaller cities as a clearing house is to local branches of banks. Most good vintage antiques pass through New York hands sooner or later. Antiques found in localities all over the country often go to New York for resale either to a few New York collectors, to customers of the major New York antiques establishments outside the city, or to successful bidders at the major auctions. To a lesser extent, this is also true of a few other major metropolitan cities in this country, but New York is *the* market place.

However, there is an increasing number of wholesalers in other geographical areas. A very large one, for example, operates two establishments in towns off the beaten track in North Carolina, selling both imported goods and antiques acquired around the countryside. Another, located on the outskirts of a medium-sized city in Tennessee, possesses a vast stock of desirable antiques ranging from art glass to seventeenth century furniture and is visited by dealers from far and wide in search of stock. In Atlanta, a wholesaler has enjoyed such increasing business, largely in stocks imported from abroad, that he has moved three times in recent years, each time into a larger building.

But the leading and the vast majority of wholesalers remain in New York City, their status and circumstances varying from that of the gentleman who inhabits an elegant mansion to that of the semi-pawnbroker in Brooklyn with a warehouse at the rear always crammed with dubious porcelain.

Among the most prosperous are those who import their antiques from overseas. For a while, their stocks were purchased primarily in England, but today there is a growing tendency to buy also in Europe, particularly from France, West Germany, Spain, and Holland. Those importers who are most successful are those who keep abreast of the American taste, which is indeed different from that in most of the older countries of the world.

At the moment, French and early American furniture are the preferences of the more sophisticated collectors. And many wealthy Americans are buying at an almost outrageous pace the paintings of British and European masters when they are available and the work of the better-known moderns. By and large, American collectors have a tendency to follow the leaders rather than to strike out on their own on new paths of collecting. When the major auction house of Sotheby Parke-Bernet Galleries, Inc., in New York City, for example, discloses, as it frequently and astutely does, record prices fetched by antiques in certain categories, there is a rush among the more wealthy collectors to acquire whatever is fetching the top prices. This tends, of course, to push prices higher still.

It is true that the best American taste is impeccable, but the rank and file of collectors like to follow style trends of the moment within their financial limitations. There exists, nevertheless, a fairly large group of more adventurous individuals who delight in pursuing such relatively new paths as those of collecting Art Nouveau or Art Deco glass and jewelry or American silver of the Victorian period or Chinese jade and bronzes.

And on the whole, 19th century furniture, ceramics, bric-à-brac and silver are far better for the mass American market today than the 17th and 18th century pieces that are the pride of British and European shops. Victorian furniture and other productions of that era were decried when only the more affluent were collecting in this country; but the ranks of collectors are swollen today with johnny-come-latelies whose ranks, in turn, embrace almost everyone from the working woman with an income and a mind of her own to newly-graduated college students to whom the Pitkin Flasks and the Sandwich glass cup plates are artifacts of an age shrouded in the mists of time.

These newer collectors appear to be consumed with a hunger for knowledge of the recent past and of the furnishings and the adjuncts that adorned the homes of their great-grandparents. They have no sneers for the awakening of the industrial age last century, or for the more intriguing and interesting products of that age, be these spool-turned beds, Rogers Groups, or cigar store Indians.

With all the wealth in this country, there are still not great numbers of Americans who can afford many examples of period Chippendale furniture, original John Singleton Copley paintings, Gobelins tapestries or 16th century Florentine bronzes, and particularly in view of the disappearing supplies of these, which tend to price them beyond the reach of all save millionaires and well-endowed institutions.

These hordes of newer collectors can, however, afford such things as Staffordshire figures and Peoria pottery, Hitchcock and Belter chairs, a variety of 19th century clocks and Wedgwood jasperware, Royal Worcester porcelain and Mettlach steins. Of such things they also are fairly hip to prices, passing by without a second glance such items in shops with price tags much above current values.

Dealers, therefore, must keep abreast of current trends in collecting, and this is as true for those who import from abroad as for those who purchase privately and at domestic sales. Several major wholesale houses in England and on the Continent are now clamoring for American trade and are making it as easy as possible for American dealers to import from them. A number of these advertise in the American collector periodicals with good results.

Some beginners and small dealers after a single glance at the customs and other regulations involved decide that importing is too complicated for them. This is myopic. The wholesalers abroad offer the utmost in cooperation, some even printing catalogues available by air mail and suggesting forwarding agents and export packers in cases in which they do not handle packing themselves.

The buyer does pay for carriage and must remember that this adds considerably to the total cost of imports. But then the packers abroad are expert at filling the empty spaces of larger pieces with smaller articles so as to cut down on trasnportation charges via ocean freight where dimensions and not weight are the factor in costs. Also, as a result of Congressional action, most antiques produced a century or more ago are now admitted duty-free into the United States. In the case of small consignments, carriage by air is often as cheap as that by far slower ship.

One wholesale firm in Lancashire, England, specializing in both the older antiques and Victoriana, catalogues 3,000 individual items and 150 quantity lines in a 200-page catalogue every ten weeks. Its catalogue subscriptions are currently $3.50 a copy via air mail with the subscription price refunded against the first purchase of $50.00 or more. It arranges on its own premises all packing and shipping details, and forwarding information is published in its catalogues. Incidentally 22-pound maximum parcel post shipments are brought direct to the door of the American purchaser.

In addition to ordering by mail from overseas, there is, of course, the possibility that you may wish, after your business has become established, to make an overseas trip and buy direct from wholesalers and others abroad. Airlines today offer tourist class fares to London and the major cities on the European continuent far lower than those in effect a few years ago. But there also is another possibility to be considered. Within the past year

or two several well-planned trips for dealers (and collectors) have
been arranged by tourist agencies and other sponsors in minimum-
fee "package" deals. A specified sum will pay for transportation
from and back to New York City, lodging and meals (or part of
the meals) abroad, overseas transportation via bus, rail, or private
cars, and gratuities. The sponsors in some instances plan full
itineraries that include visits to wholesalers, dealers, and antiques
exhibitions (including the famous flea markets of London). In
other cases, a partial itinerary is included in the deal and members of the tourist party are left other times free to go wherever
they choose.

Among these "package" deals is one known as "The Antique
Trader's Europe," featuring a series of tours covering the major
antique capitals abroad—Vienna, Brussels, Rome, Paris, and
London among them. This series was organized by Edward A.
Babka, head of the Babka Publishing Company (which publishes
The Antique Trader and *The Antiques Journal*), and Kaleido-
scope Tours. These tours are limited to participation by a
maximum of 25 persons each. The series was inaugurated in
1970.

Purchases made direct from wholesalers and others abroad
should include arrangements for transportation, but these are
easily made as has been noted above. In addition, residents
of the United States are permitted to bring back from abroad
dutiable merchandise to the value of $500 per person. Thus,
small items may be fetched home via plane or ship without difficulty or payment of duty, whether or not they fall within the
legal definition of antiques. It should be remembered that prices
of antiques abroad are rising, too, so certain purchases may not
be worth while.

It is advisable to give a further word of caution here about
purchasing damaged antiques. Unless these are so rare as to
be virtually unobtainable except in a damaged condition, they
should be left strictly alone. It is extremely difficult to sell damaged items, even at a fraction of their value, in the United States.
The majority of collectors, unfamiliar with the rarity of certain
objects from abroad, simply shun those with obvious damage;
and damage, even when not obvious, must be pointed out by the
dealer to prospective purchasers.

One thing more before concluding this chapter: we have been
asked frequently what is implied by membership in the National
Association of Dealers in Antiques, Inc.

This is a national trade association of reliable and reputable
dealers, who abide by certain moral and ethical standards of
conduct so as to command respect and confidence. Personnel in
member shops must also abide by procedures specified by
the organization, among which are the following:

Personnel in member shops will not knowingly misrepresent any item held for sale as to condition, age or authenticity.

Members agree to give a written memorandum (on request) on which will appear the selling price and a detailed description of the article sold.

Members will strive to increase their own knowledge of the arts, and encourage educational activities in behalf of the collecting public.

Members agree to price all items in dollars and cents.

Dealers may obtain applications for membership from the association's current recording secretary. Membership rosters also are available on request. The association's motto is "Antiquity with Integrity."

Applications for membership are carefully screened, and each applicant must provide references who will testify in writing as to the applicant's methods of conducting business.

This is not to say, however, that the beginning dealer or the small shop owner should consider himself in any way outside the pale if he is not a member of this organization. "His house has many mansions;" and the public undoubtedly wants all kinds of antiques shops. Possibly to refine this trade too much and develop for it semi-professional status might be to emasculate a business that has always had its essential roots and much of its attraction in the irregular.

Chapter VII

The Specialist

We have frequently advised the dealer to establish a reputation for a particular line.

Please do not think this advice envisages antiques shops converted everywhere into Madison Avenue suites with beginners sitting surrounded by careful collectors of miniatures or offering for sale only chairs made authentically by Job Townsend and John Goddard.

It is necessary that the greatest experts in this business should become specialists somewhat of this type. They perform an invaluable function at the top of the tree; and they get there only after long experience. Their lot is not necessarily a happy one, as competition is nowhere so fierce as at the top, and net profits are apt to be condemned as high when turnover is limited to the rare occasion. The specialist essentially sells direct to the collector: he must carry a large stock of which only a small percentage is sold annually. This necessitates a higher rate of profit. This is not so much immoral as inevitable.

The average antiques shop is preferably an establishment where all kinds of antiques can be bought. The general public can be frightened off by an appearance of too much specializing. The small dealer can't afford to lose urgently-needed customers because he has nothing for them. He must cater for all in order to maintain his turnover—and also in order to maintain his stock.

The disadvantage of relying upon one category of antiques for the beginning dealer is that great difficulty will be experienced in maintaining stock. Formerly, as a private collector, the beginner may have marveled at how his treasures piled up. On every trip into the country he brought another bread plate. There was no difficulty. But that collection of bread plates, acquired over long years, will be sold quickly and then the problem of replacement will become acutely insoluble. The stock for an entire shop, sufficient to provide a good turnover, cannot be maintained by purchases here and there in holiday dribbles. There has never been such an intense trade demand for top quality antiques and even for second quality ones as at present. If the beginner wisely keeps a general stock, he will at least have some furniture to sell when he has been unable to buy porcelain or glass.

All this has been said to balance what follows and to prevent the beginner from going too far on the basis of our suggestion that he should develop some specialty as a sideline or at least as a private interest as soon as possible.

This is because it is really impossible to become an expert except in one or two departments—and a reputation for a certain kind of antique is helpful in advertising and attracting customers from afar to the shop.

A little knowledge in antiques is as dangerous as in all else— dangerous to the dealer who will buy and sell wrongly, and dangerous to the customer. As we are not writing for customers in this book, we must advise the dealer to narrow down his objects of study in antiques so that he may eventually acquire some real knowledge. It is impossible for the average man to learn all there is to know about furniture, china, glass and silver, but he can become something of an expert in one of those lines after some years of study and of trial-and-error dealing.

Consequently, it is advisable to determine at the outset what will be not necessarily your specialty but your inclination—furniture, china, glass, silver, various kinds of bric-à-brac, pictures, books, primitives. Learn about the others, of course, but make your particular hobby—your bias, your prepossession, your fixation, or whatever you may choose to call it—the constant object of intensive study.

We are not writing a book on antiques as such but on operating an antiques shop, so we shall not attempt to teach the beginner about periods, styles, and values except for a concise history of furniture. Such information will be found in other books, an excellent selection of which will be found in our bibliography at the end of this volume. It is necessary to acquire a little library to learn about pottery alone. We shall, however, discuss the various classes of antiques as objects for specialty from the viewpoint of the inquiring dealer.

In furniture you can, if you wish, stock mainly oak, which is currently desired by a good many persons of moderate means for use in furnishing their homes, but bear in mind our earlier comments about oak. This will entail a cheapening of the appearance of your shop, because, as a beginner, it will be necessary to stock a considerable porportion of reproductions to meet the ordinary decorating or furnishing demands. When it comes to acquiring early true collectors' pieces in oak, your finances will probably flinch, but it is unlikely that such collectors will be numbered among your early customers. On the other hand, there is now a curious demand for 19th century oak pieces, ranging from round dining tables, to—heaven help us—cumbersome hall stands and small wash stands for the furnishing of homes. And this is as good a place as any to point out that we do not attempt to suggest what collector preferences should be: we merely report them.

Should you, however, possess a personal penchant for and interest in antique oak furniture, we suggest that you temper the timber with a bit of fruitwood, and try to cater in your shop to those furnishing cottages and small apartments. Some of the most successful beginners' shops that we know are semi-specialists in cottage or bungalow furniture, complete with the appurtenances of brass, copper and pewter, historical bottles, witch balls, and colored pottery.

Or, if the satined greys and browns of discrete walnut have always satisfied you the most, buy furniture of that kind and be prepared to cultivate a somewhat better-class trade. Such places can be associated in your shop with good glass and porcelain, chandeliers, good-quality decorative paintings, and even Oriental rugs. The same applies to mahogany furniture, possibly the most satisfying and productive for the specialist: certainly the most important at the present time. Mahogany has a wider range than walnut, with some interesting sub-specialties. We know one dealer who has established almost a corner in tea caddies, which are presently quite the rage in one section of the country. His other stock includes mahogany library and sofa tables, china cabinets, an occasional fine bookcase and bureau, and some chandeliers and porcelain.

Satinwood furniture exerts a very special appeal to a certain type of mind. It can be associated with French furniture, with mirrors and delicate porcelain, and any shop with a satinwood proclivity is beautiful almost beyond compare, though not necessarily profitable if situated in the wrong location.

With regard to French furniture as such, it is being sold in large quantities at this country's major auctions and is fetching what only a few years ago would have seemed inordinately high prices, but many of the finer pieces are going to museums and similar institutions and into the homes of wealthy private collectors. It also is stocked by the better shops in the New York and other eastern areas, but little of it is to be found in the smaller establishments in most other geographical sections of the country.

Some smaller dealers in the east also handle French furniture, and, unfortunately, some faked French pieces are to be found. Also a good bit of French furniture that is not of the period is being sold. Customers of these establishments range from firms providing props for the legitimate theatre to large stores and similar establishments whose officials like to see bergères in the basement or fauteuils in the foyers. Goods to associate with

French are French and English ceramics, clocks, glass and mirrors. Small-town dealers, however, are definitely advised to proceed cautiously with respect to stocking French—despite the fact that it remains the most splendid in antiques.

The age of rosewood, encompassing quantities of American Empire and Victorian furniture, has been much in the recent mode, and will undoubtedly be more so now that a genuine antique has been defined by our statutes as an article of merit produced just a century ago rather than one made before 1830. The shrewd commercial sense of the Americans who have been buying heavily of early, middle and even late Victorian furniture is worth noting here. They have been preparing for the day when such "junk" may command fancy prices, and indeed that day seems just around the corner. Our eyes and tastes change. Some of the better Empire and Victorian pieces now fetching fairly high prices could have been bought for a song in scores of rural areas no more than a decade or two ago. Many pieces have quadrupled in price within the past few years alone, and some have soared more than that.

Throughout this country, prices for Victorian furniture and adjuncts in general have risen considerably more percentage-wise than has the average value of antiques as a whole. Particularly important for the beginning antiques dealer are the still-increasing prices for such things as Victorian desks and early Empire secretaries; mirrors; mahogany marble-top commodes and chest of drawers; Belter mahogany couches and chairs; Gothic chairs, and library tables.

Early Victorian is undoubtedly a good specialty for the beginner to lean upon. With a keen period sense he can reconstruct a most attractive parlor of pieces considered as junk by connoisseurs of a few decades ago and maybe encourage more than a few customers to follow the increasing mode. Mounting numbers of well-established dealers are now beginning to suspect that those who so recently decried all that was Victorian did so because they visualized Victorian rooms as a whole—overcrowded with an extraordinary admixture of adjuncts and accessories— and failed to note individual pieces or to attempt to visualize individual pieces of fine craftsmanship in a different setting. We can unfortunately already foresee a new industry of faking reproduction antimacassars on backstairs looms and of offering plastic "wax" fruits for sale to embellish the apartments of aspiring movie and television stars. Thus must time march on, and, if the older generation objects, let them remember their own apprenticeship under influences that, once waxing, have waned.

Seriously, the early Victorian period in particular is an interesting, profitable and *available* period for the beginner to explore, not only with relation to its furniture but also its decorative adjuncts; and the late Victorian period can be a profitable one for those wishing to make the study of art glass their specialty.

A few years ago we would not have proceeded here with a discussion of Art Nouveau, but these are rapidly-changing times, and within the past year or two major exhibitions in this country and major auction sales have served to focus some attention upon the productions of this short-lived, somewhat fantastic but nevertheless interesting movement, which, in its creative stages, lasted only from about 1890 to 1905 but whose commercial productions continued through the outbreak of the first World War. True, these productions are not antiques but some of them have become collectible objects for which both institutions and individuals are now shelling out substantial cash. And right now the more recent Art Deco period is attracting prime interest and must be watched.

We wish merely to mention the matter here, and those who are interested or who encounter a demand for these creations in wood, glass, metals, jewelry, pottery or other substances will find reference materials for further study available.

In ceramics, the choice of specialty is between English and European porcelains, between these and American pottery, and between both and Chinese, although it is possible, and with success, to combine a study and sale of all. If this is done, then the shop should be devoted principally to china, and a steadfast decision should be made at the beginning as to whether to go after the best or become a popular emporium of cracked cups. There are sections of the country obviously unsuited to ceramic galleries and others which, by tourist influx or local taste, encourage such shops.

We would not advise the beginner or small dealer to stock very much unmarked porcelain, no matter how good the quality, unless he is certain of its provenance and is willing to guarantee its origins to his customers. Although there are specialists among collectors who know their porcelains from Adams to Zurich, they are not likely to be among your customers and the great majority of American seekers after the antique place great store by marks. Of course, many marks have been forged and others are quite undependable; nevertheless there is a penchant for marks among the uninitiate, presently constituting the bulk of those in this country who purchase collectible objects.

Certain English porcelains have always found an excellent market in the United States. These include wares from Worcester, Chelsea, Bow, Derby, Leeds, Doulton, and, of course, the productions of Wedgwood. In many localities there is an increasing demand for Chinese Export porcelain, for the better wares from manufactories in Limoges, France, and for pieces from Sèvres and Meissen. Now, too, there is emphasis on Royal Bayreuth.

But of late there has been an awakening interest in 19th century American porcelain and pottery, stemming in some measure at least from a rash of books relating to them and in part also to an intensifying national pride which is flourishing in spite of the political protests and unrest that have marked recent years. The earlier American wares, such as those made by the Tuckers and Thomas Hulme and Judge Joseph Hemphill, or Smith, Fife and Company, are exceedingly scarce and have largely disappeared into museums, but interest is being focused upon the productions at Bennington, Vermont; those created by the Robertsons at their Dedham Pottery in Massachusetts; the Deldare wares of Larkin's Buffalo Pottery; and the so-called art wares of Cincinnati's Rookwood Pottery and those of the Weller, Owens and Roseville potteries in the Zanesville, Ohio, areas. Although most of these are still well within reach of the average collector, prices of many pieces have been soaring during the past few years as interest in them has spread largely throughout the country. Soon, too, there is likely to be a reawakening of interest in the output of the Peoria (Illinois) Pottery, whose fortunes were guided at its outset by Christopher Webber Fenton of Bennington fame and for which some models were created by Bennington's outstanding designer, Daniel Greatbach.

At the moment, too, there is great interest among American collectors in such things as the Danish and other Christmas plates (including many quite recent ones which are antique in no sense but have caught the popular fancy); the work of the Havilands, both in Limoges and in the United States, which remains quite inexpensive; American historical views on English ceramics; 19th century Imari wares; the "Old Ivory" pieces from Silesia; Mettlach steins, and those wares marked "R.S. Prussia" from a factory operated by Erdman and Reinhold Schlegemilch on the edge of the Thuringen Forest. The R.S. Prussia pieces with the red star mark have tripled in price in less than five years. And, of all things, there is brisk trading right now in the handpainted Nippon trifles from Japan.

Although from the standpoints of quality and artistry, the productions of the factories mentioned above are much inferior to the high-quality English and European porcelains and pottery of an earlier era, it is in these that the heaviest trading is now being carried on and the astute dealer will do well to acquaint himself with their background so as not to be placed at a disadvantage when customers come calling for it, as they invariably will.

We hesitate to advise specialization in Oriental antiques unles one is willing to make himself an expert in the field—a chore that will require considerable study. Nevertheless, there are several Oriental specialists in this country who are doing quite well, and the dearth of imports in recent years from China has made Chinese wares in particular desirable in the eyes of collectors who view scarcity as a prime factor in rising value.

Chinese antiquities are the ultimate in collecting, satisfying a world-jaded mind as none else. Money can be and has been lost in their collection, but the dealer with a real passion for the subject possibly makes less mistakes in Chinese than in any other department. It is, however, a specialty toward which no one should be advised to lean without a genuine liking and at least a touch of the meticulous type of mind possessed by those who originally carved those jades and decorated those pristine hard-pastes.

Very much the same applies to glass, which should not be overstocked except perhaps in certain areas after experiment. The man who wants to specialize in glass has, although he may not know it, a refinement of mind almost akin to austerity; and he should be careful not to establish himself in a location where the less expensive trifles flourish. But a private interest in glass may express itself in a shop otherwise devoted to furniture most usefully, particularly if a dealer is aware of the current demand for Victorian colored art glass, almost any glass associated with the name of Louis Comfort Tiffany, and the earlier work at the Steuben Glass Works when they were under the guidance of the late Frederick Carder.

There are several flourishing shops devoted exclusively, or almost exclusively, to "art" glasses of the types known as cameo, Peach Blow, Burmese, Crown Milano, Amberina, Wavecrest, Pomona, and by various other names. Prices of these have been soaring. There also is a large and still growing demand for such things as Carnival Glass, American cut glass of the Brilliant Period (1880-1910), Custard Glass, the so-called Fairy Lamps, the molded glass of Rèné Lalique, the striped and threaded glass designed by Nicholas Lutz at the Boston and Sandwich factory and elsewhere, enameled glass of the Mary Gregory type, made in the United States and in Bohemia and elsewhere abroad, and in all types of Satin and Mother-of-Pearl wares. Also at this time there is a spreading fad for paperweights, about which dedicated collectors know considerably more than the casual dealer in them. The newest fad is for so-called Depression glass, quite unaristocratic but somehow appealing.

It is axiomatic that a certain amount of silver should be stocked by the dealer who does not wish to miss sales. Although silver can be enormously satisfying on the gracious table or as decorative adjuncts, the rise just a few years ago in the prices of silver sent collectors and speculators alike scurrying for it as an investment. English Georgian silver has been in demand for years by discriminating American collectors, but there is a parallel tendency now to collect work of American silversmiths, especially in view of new research about them. There is also in this country a large group of individuals who seek souvenir and commemorative sterling silver spoons, and their ranks are likely to swell as a result of the investigative researches into this area by Dorothy T. Rainwater and Donna H. Felger which culminated in late 1969 in the publication of their *American Spoons, Souvenir and Historical.* New interest in American silver and even silver-plate of last century has been generated by the publication of Katharine Morrison McClinton's *Collecting American Nineteenth Century Silver,* which also appeared in 1969.

If, however, the dealer becomes seriously interested in silver, he should well consider whether it may not suit him to abandon the antiques shop and become a jeweler and silversmith, quite a different type of trade, often more profitable.

There has in our time been a boom in antique jewelry, due in part to the excise tax that prevailed for some years on new jewelry as well as to the fervid buying of those who feared the worst and wanted to have their money in "something solid." With the end to inflation apparently not yet in sight despite some political pronouncements to the contrary, the antiques dealer will find it profitable to stock a few trays of Victorian rings, brooches, watches and the like, although, unless he is an expert, he should be careful of venturing beyond the semiprecious stones. If and when this demand ceases, it would be wise to clear such clutter from the shop, as it can, without judicious display and handling, impart a pawnshop or curio shop atmosphere to the most serious esablishment. Once again, jewelry is a separate business, conducted along different lines.

Pictures make a good specialty, provided the dealer has a flair for the right sort of association with antiques—colorful minor Old Masters of the Dutch and English schools, together with a sprinkling of the work of early American painters and perhaps a few American "primitives" since these of late have been rather avidly sought. It is no use indulging a wilful taste for vast and murky canvasses always bought hopefully at sales on the chance that they may turn out to be masterpieces. But persons who furnish with antiques usually require suitable wall furniture. Early 19th (and even 20th) century prints, and watercolors sell well as adjuncts to the furnishing scheme, as do intriguing old maps. It is well to be prepared for the framing of these, and some shops, in fact, do a rather good business in framing—pictures and maps, we hasten to add. The begining dealer must be advised, however, not to attempt to carry too diversified a stock of pictures because of the competition now afforded by the mushrooming of picture galleries, which sell as well as display, in almost every nook of this country. And even the department stores now tend to carry large stocks of pictures and assorted graphics.

Many other subjects for specialties could be discussed, but the primary ones have been covered. Clocks at present are experiencing a vogue, and the dealer with a good mechanical sense can buy fine old pieces with damaged movements for repairing and restoring himself. But horology is an exact science, pitted with falls, for the overconfident.

The beginner may indeed swing far from the beaten track without profit. A well-known dealer who is a leading buyer of the best paperweights was probably an eccentric when he started. We know another dealer whose backyard is a litter of old iron: he sells early agriculture implements, and one of his customers is a famous film star who delights in pointing out to visitors the collection of plows in his lounge.

Chapter VIII

Income Taxes, Etc.

Antiques dealers who maintain shops are assessed for income and business taxes just as are other shopkeepers, and they will need to keep meticulous records against the day when they may find themselves confronted with a demand from the sleuths of the Internal Revenue Bureau for proof of income and outgo.

The private dealer is in a more advantageous position. There have been cases in which he has paid no income tax at all—until the Bureau of Internal Revenue or his State Income Tax Division has caught up with him (as they nearly always do).

If an individual occasionally buys and sells antiques in his spare time, he is technically required to report his profit on his individual income tax returns.

This applies with special rigor to those individuals who have no physical shop as such but who sell antiques from their homes, many of them through the mail order business. The individual who makes an occasional sale of one of his own antiques does not need a special business license but should report his profit on his income tax forms. On the other hand, most municipalities and country governments that levy business license taxes—and most of them do—require that such a license be obtained and that inventory taxes be paid when such an individual goes out and buys any stock of goods and then brings them into his home specifically for the purpose of sale.

The revenue departments of various municipal, county, and state governments have their own interpretations of conducting a business, and the dealer should obtain from them a knowledge of just what their regulations and requirements are. Those in the business of regularly buying and selling antiques are subject to the same regulations, with respect to taxes generally, as are those most other regular business involving buying and selling. The majority of incorporated cities and towns as well as many counties towns require that a business license be obtained and that a fee be paid for it. In many cases, however, the amount of the fee depends upon the type of business. Many local governments impose an inventory tax upon the value of merchandise on the dealer's floor as of the first day of each year.

Federal income taxes are almost universally applicable today, although there are still a few states that do not impose state income taxes. Consequently, the private dealer who negotiates many transactions annually for a livelihood will be wise to make a correct report of his income; otherwise the day will come when a jealous competitor or a hawk-nosed investigator for a state or the federal government will undo him. Such a dealer will then find all his transactions over past years laid bare. He will have to pay an accountant or a lawyer to handle the case, and he will have to pay an excess amount in addition to the original taxes due plus a fine, and there are terms of imprisonment for fraudulent practices. Unless the individual possesses nerves of steel, moreover, he will find that worry over exposure will not be worth the gold under the floor boards.

The best attitude toward taxation is to pay after claiming proper exemptions and expenses and then, if you think the taxation too heavy, support actively a political party that aims to reduce taxation by economy in government spending. It may be well to point out here, however, that a search for such a party in these days may be long if not entirely fruitless.

As an antiques dealer, you will pay tax to the Federal Government on your net profit for each year. The net profit is determined by totaling your gross receipts or sales and then subtracting specified allowable deductions.

On your income tax return you will list the value of your inventory at the beginning of the year; the amount you spent for the purchase of goods for sale (less the value of any such goods withdrawn for personal use); your costs for labor, materials and supplies for the shop; then subtract from this total the value of your inventory at the end of the taxable year. This permits you to determine the cost of the goods you sold. Your gross profit is then determined by subtracting this cost of goods so sold from your gross receipts or sales for the year.

From your gross profit, you may then deduct such expenses as depreciation for the vehicle you bought for use in connection with your shop; the business license taxes you paid; your rent on the shop premises; sums paid for repairs, insurance, and legal or professional fees and commissions (if any); bad debts, and any losses on your business property. You then subtract these total allowable expenses from your gross profit to determine your net profit, which is the amount upon which you are taxed.

Federal income tax regulations and rates are, however, like the clothing in your washing machine, in a constant state of flux, so that you will probably find it worth while to employ an accountant to help you with checking your records of sales and expenses and preparing your return.

Cerainly you should keep accounts carefully in a book with several columns on each side, obtainable from any business stationer. You should list in this book your receipts and your payments, including payments for stock and all allowable expenses. Your allowable expenses, incidentally also include amounts spent for advertising, utilities, janitorial service, essential travel in connection with operation of the business, and so on.

Make certain that you obtain an invoice for every purchase you make in connection with the business and for other expenses and that you retain all your paid and cancelled checks made out in payment for these things.

The Federal Internal Revenue Bureau has employees who will help you with your tax problems. If, however, you are new to business, it will probably be more advantageous to employ an accountant, who will go through the records you have kept, your receipts and your disbursements and will prepare a balance sheet and/or profit and loss statement for you to submit with your income tax forms to the Internal Revenue Bureau and also to your State Internal Revenue Bureau in states in which payment of income taxes is required. He will, of course, charge you a fee for this service, its amount depending upon the work involved and the time necessary for it, but you are likely to find the fee quite reasonable in comparison with the headaches involved in the preparation of your own returns.

Should you conduct your business from a house or shop in which you also live, then you are permitted to deduct a proportionate share of such things as rent, utilities, insurance, and depreciation, the balance being allocated to your personal living expenses, which are not deductible.

Should you hire employees to work for you, then you must also deduct from their pay the Federal "pay as you go" income taxes (and also such state taxes where applicable) as well as Social Security taxes. The amount of these taxes, you must turn in to the Federal Government (and where applicable, to the State Government). The amounts to be withheld by you from employees' pay are based upon the total amount of the wages or salaries together with the number of of exemptions to which the employees are entitled. Social Security taxes withheld must be matched by you, the employer. The Government will furnish you with tax tables which show the amounts to be withheld for each pay period. At the end of each year, you must furnish employees with a statement showing their total wages for the year and the amount you have withheld for taxes.

Sales taxes constitute still another headache for the shop keeper. Such taxes, in varying percentages, are now imposed by most of the States and also in some instances by municipalities. You must collect sales taxes from the purchasers of your goods and, in turn, pay the proper percentage to the State and/or municipal government. Forms for computing this tax will be provided you by the governmental agencies involved and these must be filled out and returned to these agecnies, together with payments due, by specified dates. Otherwise, you will incur penalties.

As each year draws toward its tangled end, it would be well for you to try to determine your profits, and, if they appear to involve you in a heavy tax payment, to consider whether it might not be wise to spend at once a portion of them on advertising, which is a deductible expense, and which enables you to reinvest a part of your earnings in yourself.

We proceed from this very brief discussion of taxation to a consideration of points that bear on it, among which a very pertinent one is the question of what legal status should be self-imposed on your business—that of a one-man concern (or sole proprietorship), a partnership, or a corporation. If you are on your own, of course, no question of partnership can arise, but should you join forces with another person, either as an active or an inactive partner, then it must be considered whether or not a formal agreement be drawn up. If it is decided to embark upon a partnership, then a written and properly-witnessed agreement should be prepared.

A partnership is the simplest kind of business for two or more persons to start and end. The partners are taxed separately and all partners except *limited* partners are personally liable for debts.

A corporation operates under state laws, has a continuous legal life, and the business's profit are taxed separately from the earnings of the officials or executive and owners. In a corporation, the company itself and not the owners or operators are liable for debts and taxes of the firm. A corporation operates under a charter which restricts its scope of activity and its name.

The antiques shop operator should familiarize himself with the advantages and disadvantages of the three main types of business— the proprietorship, the partnership, and the corporation—and if, after starting as a sole proprietorship, he wants to consider the other possibilities, he should certainly consult a lawyer. Briefly, however, here are some pertinent features of partnerships and corporations.

A general partnership agreement may be established by the signing of a partnership agreement by the executives. Actually, either a written or an oral agreement is effective, but, as we have just stated, a written agreement is preferable since there is less likelihood of misunderstanding arising.

A limited partnership is somewhat different from a general partnership. To form one, it is necessary to file a written contract with the proper official of your State, and the contract must incorporate certain legal requirements. Such a contract enables one to limit the liability of one or more of the partners to the actual amount they invested in the business. However, in addition to the limited partners, at least one general partner also must be specified. In addition, all limited partners must invest in the business either in the form of cash or tangible property. And the State in which you reside has certain laws and regulations relating to limited partnerships to which you must conform.

Corporations may be formed only by following the legal procedures set up by the individual State Government. Articles of incorporation must be filed with the State, and filing fees and an initial tax must be paid. After this, stockholders must meet to complete the formal organization, including the adoption of bylaws and, election of a board of directors and officers.

Some States require a specific amount of the par value of the capital stock to be paid in cash and put in the bank before a certificate of incorporation is submitted to the State.

Corporation laws and charter fees vary considerably from State to State.

No matter what type of legal structure you adopt, you should remember that your business creditors are invariably entitled to be paid out of the business assets before any equity capital may be withdrawn; and where such assets are insufficient, the type of business organization you have selected will determine the extent to which the owner or owners can be forced to supply creditors' claims out of their invdividual funds.

In the case of an individual proprietorship, the proprietor personally is liable for all his business's debts, and to the extent, if necessary, of all the property he owns. In a general partnership, each partner is personally liable for all debts owed by this partnership without regard to the amount of his individual investment. However, in the case of a limited partnership, the limited partners risk only the loss of the capital they have invested, although the general partners in such an operation are liable individually and jointly for all debts.

Corporations do possess a risk advantage, since creditors' claims ma   enforced to the limit of the company's assets only. If those assets are not sufficient to meet all claims, the shareholder still does no have to delve into his personal pocket.

The Small Business Administration, an agency of the United States Government, supplies aid and advice in various forms to many small businesses, including publications that may be helpful. One such publication deals with the matter of selecting the best legal structure for a firm. Another relates to the steps involved in incorporation a business. These particular publications are available without charge from any of the numerous field offices this agency has established throughout the country.

Since there are both advantages and disadvantages in any type of legal business structure, we reiterate that professional advice should be obtained, and whatever suggestions have been made by us here are not intended as a substitute for professional advice.

A word may be added about insurance. It is best to take out a comprehensive policy with a company recognized by and regulated by the state in which you are located. The policy should cover all stock in the shop as well as any stock in transit. A policy should also protect the shopkeeper from liability for personal injuries that may be sustained by others on his premises. The small dealer will likely find, however, that the cost of including protection against loss by breakage is prohibitive. Should the stock be very valuable, it could be advantageous to adopt such a safeguard against theft as the installation of a burgler alarm system. May companies install such systems, which are electronically operated, charging you an installation fee plus a monthly fee for servicing it. The installation company retains ownership of the system and the shopkeeper, in effect, merely leases it. There are some alarm systems that may be purchased outright, but most of these are relatively expensive. Insurance costs also can be held down by the installation of metal burglar bars across doors and windows through which a burgler might overwise effect entry. Here, too, a considerable amount of expense may be involved. Your insurance agent will advise you as to the costs and provisions of all types of business insurance policies.

You may wish to consider what is known in the trade as a "fine arts" policy. This is often less expensive than a comprehensive policy and will cover fully the contents of your shop against loss. However, such a policy does entail considerable book work, since the insurer normally requires a listing of individual items and their value.

At any rate, you should always keep a "stock book," recording all pieces bought and values, so that insurance claims can be supported by proper evidence.

Chapter IX

Antiques Dealers

This book started with a consideration of personal qualities required for dealing in antiques. It cannot continue on a better theme than that of the individual dealer—a study more fascinating to some collectors than the actual collection of antiques itself. We doubt whether any trade or profession today contains such a variety of individuality as antiques dealing, wherein the twin factors of artistic temperament and freedom from rules and agreed conventions promote singularity of character and some most extaordinary juxtapositions, as of a saintly man partnered with his brother, a roughneck and a roysterer. There are aristocrats in junk shops and former pickers in New York salons.

A brief excursion into experience here may not only provide an entertaining end to this book but also furnish some useful tips to the reader.

The average antiques dealer in the United States today is frankly a delightful person to know. Somehow or another, the association with fine craftsmanship, objects of beauty, and also with discriminating customers tends to soften coarseness of the mind and make for ease and pleasantness in society.

We remember strong coffee sipped from heavy mugs in the dark recesses of an old shop with an elderly woman of Romany descent, surrounded by odd characters from the neighborhood, and we remember learning quite a lot about porcelain in the process. We remember an ex-Marine selling antiques lovingly under the shade of a huge oak tree at an outdoors festival in Georgia; an old man scarcely able to write his name but with a knowledge of antiques that was little short of astonishing; a former sailor who has become a leading authority on pictures and who, from his shop in Hawaii, "discovered" a talented painter and nurtured him to fame; a former advertising executive whose keen commercial sense makes him a byword for bargains in all furnishings antiques. This applies all over the world but particularly in England and America.

A lovely white-columned mansion in the country may mask a considerable antiques business conducted by solid folks of the hunting type, who reveal that their manners may be out-moded and their background obsolete but the old indomitable spirit that originally built the mansion is still there.

One of the most fascinating but not necessarily up-to-date shops in the South is to be found in a relatively small community in Tennessee in which there are situated probably more an-tiques shops than any other single type of business. This is pre-sided over by a gentleman who gives the impression of having stepped out of the pages of a book and who shows visitors around with a soft but firm intent, cold and distant if crossed or taken less than seriously, warm and brilliant if in contact with a kindred spirit. The commodious spaces in his rambling one-story shop reveal an amazing variety of stock. There are areas piled with treasures, among which colored glass in memory semes to invest the scene with a kaleidoscopic light. One large room is crowded with furniture of the type that is currently in demand. He knows what is selling, and his prices are right.

And memory leaps across space and time to a business in Atlanta which consists of no more than one big overcrowded, dingy room, wherein an elderly woman seems continually to be wrapping and unwrapping articles of begrimed porcelain and glass until the whole space is a sea of cardboard and old newspapers.

Some of the most interesting dealers with whom to talk are those whose fathers and even grandfathers were in the trade before them. Such dealers seem possessed of a quiet assurance of manner that is indeed different from the pretentious self-assurance of some others, and the knowledge they impart in their quiet but straightforward manner is sound.

The type most disliked—and their numbers, alas, are grow-ing—are the Philistines who march through competitors' shops, banging tables briskly and saying, "How much? I'll give you half," or belittling what they encounter and offering to take it off the proprietor's hands for a fraction of its value. But it is often found that even some of these have an interesting side when their masks can be lowered by familiarity—and your worth revealed to them.

There are large companies that operate antiques businesses with many subsidiary shops and a multiplicity of agents and pickers across the country; there are businesses run in side streets by impoverished widows of desceased dealers; there are chromium-fronted shops and shops unaltered even to the cobwebs since the days of William Tecumseh Sherman, who attained fame by strik-ing more matches than any man of his times.

One well-known name in the business is that of a man who some years ago began a weekend antiques business in a barn behind his home in a rural community and then along the way accumulated enough capital and "know-how" to expand until today he controls an entire "antiques village" of more than 30 shops, all of which he built himself on his own premises. In this field he was a pioneer, and today the "antiques supermarkets" with a dozen or a score or more of shops under the same roof are beginning to flourish.

There is a young man in a quiet city, son of a father who once sold antiques to Henry Ford and J. P. Morgan, who was largely responsible himself some years ago when little more than a boy for initiating the fashion for Regency. He sells now to the contemporary equivalents of his father's great names; his father kept him severely at work in the packing room and at the workbench as a boy.

There is a young woman who presides over a city beer parlor in the evenings after the days spent in her own country shop, where she specializes in bottles, a subject about which she has written several books.

We know a termite exterminator who sells and repairs antique clocks, more for the joy of it than the profit, and a grocer who, perhaps appropriately enough, deals in pot lids on the side. A large general hardware store has an excellent antiques department, which means more to the owner of that establishment than all the other more lucrative departments. Many proprietors of country restaurants sell antiques, some by the expedient of decorating their establishments with them and selling off the walls. We know of a partnership between a wealthy businessman and the elderly lady proprietor of a second-hand shop with clothes hanging outside. The businessman provides the capital and the old lady buys antiques which are displayed in another shop—delightful French antiques.

There is a flourishing shop specializing in furniture housed in a vast two-story barn in a rural area so remote that it is difficult to find without a map. There is one street in a metropolitan city with money flowing past the doors each day, where the little shops seem to change hands almost every week.

It is possible to enter a certain shop in a university village in North Carolina and to talk with the proprietor and his wife on an equal footing whether you be a professor or a professional boxer, and to talk of metaphysics, poetry, football, and the strange fate of man.

Languishing ladies linger in some shops under fringed lampshades; in others there are buxom women who will tell your fortune. An exiled Russian prince is to be found here, a former magnate of Vienna there.

A one-time gay proprietor of a widely-known night club presides today over an antiques business besides a small creek far from the madding crowd. Another time you may be talking, although you do not always know it, to a famous artist who manages a small shop. The mistress of a Colonial mansion in one of the most beautiful villages in the country has the antiques shop therein; and the proprietor of a large shop who has a magnificent house at the back and knows more of beauty than half a dozen connoisseurs combined calls his customers "Buddy"!

It would be wrong, however, to leave the reader with the impression that the general run of dealers is eccentric or somehow fabulous. The average man is middle-aged with considerable sensibility, taste, and ease of manner. He does not ignore or push his customers, and his efforts are dedicated toward being honest as well as successful, attributes which are not as incompatible as the cynics think. He runs a business in New England, where you may often pick up scarce souvenir spoons or fine old maps (his private interests). Or he is to be found in a small establishment in Colorado, handling porcelain which he has, on more than one occasion, displayed in museums. Maybe in the barren reaches of Nevada he may be found, proud of his early American chairs, or beneath the shadow of a textile mill in South Carolina, advertising for miniatures.

He is shrewd about money, and naturally quick to pick up the salient points of a piece, but not miserly and seldom afflicted with knowledge to such an extent that he cannot buy save at rare occasions and at Parke-Bernet.

When you enter his shop, you may find that he is away and that his wife is there instead, a woman who can talk but not too much, bargain but not bicker, and whose influence in the business is obviously to brighten and refine.

Or, on the contrary, you may find that *she* is away and that her husand is there instead, for in the United States in recent years increasing numbers of women have entered the fray, not as assistants to their husbands but as proprietors. By no means all, but a majority of the shops owned wholly or in part by women tend to specialize in the daintier antiques. Whereas the male of the species prefers furniture and such things as mechanical banks, steins, and weapons, the female finds herself enchanted more with lovely porcelains, glass, and perhaps fans and dolls.

Yet there are women in this business who can do an expert job of refinishing furniture and wiring lamps. And, by and large, their advice about furnishing and decorating is pertinent and often finds the ready ear of female customers and not infrequently of the male as well.

One feminine antiques shop proprietor we know has a flourishing sideline specialty of framing prints, and the revenue she derives from this is nearly equal to that obtained from the sale of antiques. Another, has a sideline specialty of wiring appropriate antiques for lamps, and in her stock she carries a variety of objects that may be converted into lighting devices. The fact is that there are apparently few objects indeed which ingenious ladies do not think they can turn into lamps, some, alas, in much the same manner in which her fairy godmother turned Cinderella into a princess. Nevertheless, at least in this country, the conversion of miscellaneous objects into lamps is a thriving enterprise, and the lady in question is making a good thing of it.

Generally, too, the small or beginning shops operated by women or in which the feminine influence is present are more attractive physically than those operated exclusively by beginning males. The junk shop atmosphere still lingers here and there in the antiques business, but it does not hold quite the fascination it may once have for the well-to-do collector. Feminine customers for decorative adjuncts, for example, prefer to see these accessories displayed in appropriate settings, and here is where so many female dealers shine.

Then, too, women normally keep better abreast of fads and fashions in home furnishing than do men; consequently, they are on the alert for antiques that address themselves to the demands of the day. While they may have their own preferences, they remain sensitive to the preferences of their customers and therefore tend to buy things that will sell and to eschew those that may, regardless of intrinsic merit, chiefly accumulate dust.

All told, today's antiques dealers are a fine lot, their judgment and their integrity respected by their customers. And, in a day in which innovation, change for its own sake, and revolt are the philosophy of so many, the antiques dealer is really among the few true conservatives left—if conservatism seeks to preserve the best of the past amid the raw turmoil of the future.

Museum curators, history teachers, and librarians are not enough. They tend to preserve the best of the past in a vacuum which has little or no influence upon everyday life. The dealer in antiques carries the tradition of the ages into the market place and thus into the hubbub of the home itself. He or she guides us not only in our furnishings but also in our choice of a background for living. And the manner of a life is largely determined by its background.

Neat, attractive, picturesque shops like this one attract antiquers.

Chapter X

A Pocket History of Furniture

Because furniture still remains the staple commodity for aggregate dollar sales in the antiques business, a concise history of furniture and its development may be helpful to the beginning dealer.

The history of art in furniture and allied crafts begins many thousands of years ago with the Egyptians. There was, of course, furniture long before that, or the Egyptian variety would not have been so well developed, but our adequate records go pack only to the Egyptians. There are still to be seen in museums some remarkable specimens of furniture in colored wood found in the tombs of the Pharaohs.

This earliest furniture in our possession should cure us of any great pride we might take in our own development of the art, as it is almost excessively "modern" in method of construction, being based mainly on the principle of the pylon, with a beautiful simplicity as the keynote of the design, and with a lavish use of "modern" color. The Egyptians knew all the crafts of carving and inlaying; they used many different woods with a special predilection for cedar, as well as ivory, metals and colored glass. The inlaying of ivory in ebony was a favorite method—long before Charles André Boulle.

So, with the salutary reminder that history is not necessarily progress, we can pass to the Babylonians and Assyrians, who have left us some massive examples of thrones executed in such enduring if not endearing substances as basalt and bronze, and we may note that a stone carving of an Assyrian throne in the British Museum shows legs of very similar design to products of the French Empire period at its fag-end.

The ancient Jews, with their contemporaries, the Medes and the Persians, evidently used furniture of a more enduring quality and a rather more considerable richness than that in favor in

73

the present day. Beds made of wood inlaid with ivory and gold
were in use as early as the 13th century B.C. The Bed of Solomon,
as it well might be, was constructed of cedar of Lebanon, with
pillars of silver and bottom of gold. The bed of Og, King of
Bashan, was nine cubits long by four feet wide and was of
iron. It might be significant indeed that when the Bible and other
writings of the period describe furniture, they usually mention
beds. The following description of a bedchamber is taken from
the *Book of Esther*:

> "White, green and blue hangings, fastened with cords
> of fine linen and purple, to silver rings and pillars of
> marble: the beds were of gold and silver."

So we come to the Greeks, and a very different conception
of interior decoration. According to the authority Whibley, "Greek
houses were probably very bare. . . . Beyond beds and couches,
chairs, stools, footstools and small portable tables, they do not
seem to have had anything that we should call furniture—except
chests." This statement is, however, misleading, as the Greeks
did produce some of the most beautiful furniture ever devised,
the clean lines of which, as shown in extant statues and friezes,
excel anything attempted by "modern" functionalists.

The Greek chair known as the *klismos* was a perfect example
of elegance combined with simplicity. There are long periods in
the history of furniture which are dismal, pretentious and hope-
lessly inefficient by comparison. The *klismos* had a back consisting of a deep, concave rail resting on two side supports, and
four legs, the front pair curving forwards and the others back-
wards.

Many chairs of the Empire period were founded on this model.
The Greeks also developed the couch to a degree of perfection
never since excelled. They had a charming way with low occasional
tables. They used such timber in their furniture as oak, cedar,
cypress, sycamore, pine, fig, box, and ebony.

The Romans took Greek furniture, as they took other Greek
ideas and possesions, and elaborated it, not always to advantage.

"English" furniture falls, according to the pundits, into the
following periods: Celtic, Roman, Anglo-Saxon, Norman, Gothic
Rennaissance (Elizabethan and Jacobean), Carolean, 18th century, 19th century, Edwardian and "modern."

We know little of the Celtic period, save that it produced
remarkably fine metal work: the earliest ancestors of the English
must have made some very interesting furniture also; but in this
brief survey it is best to proceed past the Roman period, when
Britons momentarily saw such domestic interiors as they would
not know again for a thousand years, to the Anglo-Saxon, which
is familiar today mainly through illuminated manuscripts.

In the Anglo-Saxon period it appears that furniture was strictly utilitarian. The trestle table was used, and households of high degree might boast a round table. There is a manuscript that shows such a table, the top of which must have turned upon a hinge. Chairs were mainly benches and stools. Beds were usually bags of straw on benches or chests. It was not until the Norman Conquest that any considerable art creeps into the furniture of that time: the Normans developed the Romanesque and then Gothic. Romanesque art, characterized by the rounded arch, was well known to the Saxons, but the finest fruits were ripened for England in Normandy, and William's followers in due course welcomed and patronized the great products of the Gothic period.

Henry III (1216-1272) introduced the paneling of rooms into England. Chests or coffers (also called lockers, arks, hutches) now came into prominence as the most important single article of furniture used for nearly all purposes, as receptacles, seats, panelled and carved, and fastened together by wood pegs and interlocking wood joints.

Furniture surviving from the medieval period is of oak. Beech, elm, deal, and chestnut were used also, but these timbers perished and only oak survives from the period. Thus it can be judged whether a chest is genuinely medieval. A further test is the grain of the oak, which was always made to appear in diagonal splashes which rise above the softer surface with age, and which appear lighter or darker in color according to the angle of viewpoint. It was a wasteful way of cutting oak, but they had plenty in those days. The modern faker cannot manage it.

Again, the medieval touch is shown in the use of decorative ironwork at hinges and strengthening bands. This is heavy and sumptuous, and never to be mistaken. In any case, only a few genuine products of the period remain, and these are mostly in English museums and churches.

The evolution of the chest or coffer could indeed be identified wholly with the history of English furniture. In the 13th century coffers were made with backs and arm-pieces at either end, the first settles. These developed eventually into armchairs, settees, and the great settles still to be found in farmhouses in Britain.

Also from this period of the birth of panelling in England is derived the "dressoir," at first a panelled cupboard for keeping food. It became a separate article of furniture, permanently open at the front, in which the number of shelves, used for displaying plate, indicated the rank of the owner. A cloth would be laid on the top of the lower part of the dressoir at meal times.

An important development of the history of panelling, which should be known to those wishing to identify periods exactly, is the appearance of the "linen-fold" pattern in the 15th century.

It was introduced from Flanders and lasted about 80 years, being found in England until 1550.

The periods of the Renaissance (Tudor, Elizabethan, Jacobean) were the product of the arrival in England of Continental notions of art based on the rediscovery of Roman and Greek designs wedded to Gothic forms. They were characterized by an insistence on formality and rigid pattern, by the return of the rounded arch in architecture, and by a decorative sophistication, which culminated in decoration for its own sake.

The chest soon began to show signs of the new influences. Chests surviving from the period of Henry VIII are often decorated in front with elaborate architectural designs in inlaid work: these are sometimes known as "Nonesuch" chests, from the name of Henry's great palace near Ewell in Surrey—and now the oaken chair evolved from the chests became finally and completely an article of furniture in its own right.

The cross-framed type of chair was developed at this time, often of walnut, and with leather bands to form back and seat. Chairs of turned work, often called "thrown" chairs, were introduced, and continued to be made until the end of the 17th century.

Meanwhile, the trestle table was still used, but was finally superseded by the framed table in the middle of the 16th century. Oak was the most generally used wood, and continued so until 1660, but walnut had begun to find favor, and cherry was frequently used. This was a wood that became a deep coffee color with age. Panelling proceeded apace, now called wainscotting (from the Dutch "Wagenschot," meaning oak). Varnish had to wait until the middle of the 16th century, and wood surfaces were still treated mainly with wax polish or oil.

The primary characteristic of the Elizabethan period was heavy elaboration of the tendencies so far described. Furniture became more and more architectural, heavy and much burdened with extraneous, often grotesque, decoration. Yet the development was successful in that it attained an individuality of beauty which has persisted in spite of all changes since, and which is still the obvious ideal of nine-tenths of Englishmen, as may be seen by a walk through the London suburbs.

The framed table appeared with its first great baluster legs joined by four heavy rails near to the floor. The expanding table was developed, with sliding leaves at either end. Others were made with tops that could be turned up on hinges and frames that could then be used as seats. Tables were introduced with chess or tric-trac (background) boards marked on top and drawers below to hold chessmen and other pieces. Chairs meanwhile continued to be made with solid panelled backs, usually of oak (a custom which continued until the time of William and Mary). Furniture mounts were usually of heavy hammered iron.

With the Jacobean period the heaviness began to be mitigated by a lighter fancy, but the strong individuality of Tudor furniture was correspondingly diminished. It became the custom to apply ornament rather than to carve it from the original. Silk and velvet came into fashion for upholstery and draping, so that artistry in the actual fashioning of the woodwork of furniture was less important.

Jacobean tables no longer have exaggerated legs, as the Elizabethan type. Indeed, the most characteristic article of furniture of the period of James I and Charles I is the gate-legged table with legs of turned work, which now became so popular. (This twisted turned work came from Holland, where it was in turn imported from the East by Dutch traders.)

It was during the reign of Charles I in Great Britain that the first furniture of the transatlantic colonies began to emerge, and it was natural that the first stylistic influence on American craftsmen was that of the English working in the Jacobean style. The early pieces made on these shores were simple, constructed of solid wood, sturdy, and the joined pieces held in place by wooden pegs.

The Jacobean influence on the American craftsmen extended from shortly after the arrival of the Pilgrims in 1620 throughout most of the 17th century. The earliest pieces made were chests, boxes, chairs, tables, and a few press and court cupboards. The earliest chests, urgently needed for storage, were made of oak but a little later the backs, bottoms and even front panels (customarily three in number) were made from hard pine. Decoration was largely by carving in a style borrowed from the Flemish and by the application of split spindles and knoblike bosses cut in the shape of lozenges or diamonds.

Probably the first chests were made without drawers, but a good many with drawers also survive today. The legs, at first a continuation of the corner stiles (or vertical end members) extended several inches below the flat chest bottom, and later ended in ballshaped feet. When drawers were added, there were only one or two in the bottom; those with more drawers are rare.

A well-known name to connoisseurs is that of the Hadley chest, named after a town in Massachusetts from which many of the type are said to have come. They are characterized by shallow carving of designs of tulips, leaves and vines over the entire front surface. They had three sunken panels of rectangular shape across the front.

Another noted type is the Connecticut sunflower chest, also made with three front panels but boasting a middle panel carved with designs resembling the flower for which it is named. Carved tulips usually embellish the other two panels. Additional ornamentation included turned split spindles glued to the upper front surface, between and at the ends of the panels, and, frequently, on the stiles at the ends of the drawers, and also bosses glued to the drawer fronts.

These low storage chests were succeeded late in the century by chests of drawers, made in much the same manner of construction except that the tops were made fast instead of being hinged. These chests were, in effect, wooden cases, primarily of oak, with solid sides and backs and with drawers inserted in their fronts. Drawer handles were usually turned wooden knobs, although occasionally iron or brass drops were used. Some chests of drawers had feet that were an extension of the stiles; others were made with ball-shaped feet.

Some of the more pretentious homes of our Pilgrim ancestors boasted court (or livery) and press cupboards. The former reflected the form of the English buffet and was used to hold plate, glass and commonplace eating utensils. They were customarily made of two sections. The cupboard of the top half was set back from the front and contained one or more compartments for storage, and, often, one or two drawers. There was an overhanging cornice at the top with turned posts at the front corners. The bottom half had an open shelf with turned posts or columns at the front corners and the shelf itself only a few inches above floor level. The familiar split spindles and bosses were sometimes used as decoration.

Press cupboards contained either an additional cupboard or drawers in the lower portion so they could be used as a linen-press. Some authorities, including Luke Vincent Lockwood, think the terms "court" and "press" cupboards were used interchangeably in this country and that both referred to the latter type.

The use of chairs was limited largely until the final quarter of the 17th century to persons of importance. The rank and file of the Colonists when indeed they found time to sit at all sat on joined stools or benches. Chairs made until the mid-17th century were of either the wainscot or turned type. The experts say that the earliest chairs were made with three legs. A famous one of this type known as the "Harvard" chair is thought to be of English workmanship. These three-legged chairs had two legs at front, one at back. Support for the back was provided by arms extending from the front post and by the upward projection of the leg at back. Apparently a good many were made with spindles in their backs.

Wainscot chairs, of oak, were close to massive with backs that were framed and paneled and, frequently, carved. Seats were made of solid wood and legs were braced. Joints were of the mortise-and-tenon type, fastened with pins.

Similar to such chairs in basic design were Wainscot table-chairs with tall, movable backs that could be swung forward across an arm to provide a table.

Famous among the early American chairs are those known as the Carver and Elder Brewster types. These were named after two gentlemen who came over on the Mayflower—John Carver and William Brewster. An original Carver chair, said to have been brought over from England by John Carver (who was elected first governor of Plymouth Colony) is now preserved in Pilgrim Hall at Plymouth. The Carver chairs have four legs and usually three horizontal rails and the same number of vertical spindles in the back. They have simple turned posts with knobs and rush seats.

The Brewster chair has a double tier of four vertical turned spindles in back, three rows of similar ones on each side under the arms, and two rows in the front below the seat.

There was also a Cromwellian chair, styled after those made during the Puritan domination of England (1649-1660) and characterized by severity of line and lack of decoration. There was an austere straight frame, leather seat, and a strip of leather or of some textile across the back. Not many of this type, however, were made on these shores.

Other 17th century American chairs included turned slat-backs (the slats were horizontal), and cane chairs with seats and a part of the backs fashioned of cane. Some high-backed cane chairs boasted fine carving and turning.

Not many 17th century tables survive. The earliest one known is dated 1650 and is preserved in the Metropolitan Museum of Art. The type is known as board-on-a-frame or trestle and consists of a long flat pine board supported on a frame of oak trestles. Other tables included the gateleg, Wainscot types with heavy bracing, and the chair-table mentioned earlier.

In addition to small dining tables, there were tavern tables, the simplest of which were made with a board top on a frame with posts or legs at the four corners, held in place by stretchers. In later tavern tables one or two drawers were added in the apron below the top. Other small tables were made with twisted legs or stretchers, or with raked legs and leaves supported by boards of winglike shape fastened to the stretchers in such a way that they could be pivoted ("butterfly" tables). Woods used in tables included oak, pine, walnut and maple.

Day beds with adjustable backs also appeared in the 17th century. Heads were in the shape of chair backs and seats were extended to bed length. Most had eight legs. The adjustable head was operated by means of attached straps or chains which enabled one to tilt it forward or backward. These early ones had caned seats and backs.

The ordinary bed, however, consisted primarily of a wooden frame with either ropes or wooden slats to support a mattress of cloth-covered straw or feathers. Many families used curtains around these, both for privacy and for protection from drafts.

Other 17th century furniture made in America included trundle beds, Bible and desk boxes (and a few other types), candle stands, cradles, desk boxes on frames, settles, chests on frames, and occasionally desks on frames.

Toward the close of the Resoration period in England the idea of luxury and ostentation there soared until it reached the fantastic height of the silver table. Several of these extraordinary pieces are preserved at Windsor, Knole and in British museums. Their fashion came from Versailles, and silver was also used in the manufacture of chair frames, fire dogs, candle sconces and brackets.

At the same time, the art of japanning arrived in England from the East via Holland, nad the long fashion for "Chinese" decoration was begun. Indeed, this was the age of plastering, varnishing and veneering. Walnut veneer rapidly became popular; about 1675-1680 the art was elaborated still further by marquetry, again first brought to fine fruition in Holland after Dutch merchants had observed work of this kind in India.

Thus the Carolean period is succeeded briefly by the era of William and Mary, during which the future course of English (and also American) furniture was set by the accident of the arrival of the Court of Orange in London with all its strongly individual preferences in design. It was, indeed, a brief succession, for the reign did not last long, and the Dutch styles as such did not appeal sufficiently to endure in their complete form. But the furniture of William and Mary, wedded to the traditional furniture of the Jacobean and Carolean periods, produced as redoubtable offspring the famous styles of the 18th century.

Two main features of the Dutch furniture chiefly influenced the furniture of England and the American Colonies. The first was the heavy solid design, particularly marked in cabriole legs, bombé sides and fronts, and simplicity of background. The second was the use of lacquer and varnish, veneer and marquetry.

Possibly the stout legs and the marquetry left their mark the longest. The chairs that made designers such as Chippendale so famous were all solidly based on Dutch legs to begin with: the marquetry never became widely popular, but remained as a uniquely beautiful contribution to the mainstream of furniture.

The William and Mary style arrived in the American Colonies a few years after it had begun to be made in England, and the use of oak gave way to that of walnut as the preferred wood. Among the notable new pieces new pieces of furniture introduced during the reign of William and Mary were highboys (called "tall boys" in England) and lowboys, which also seems to be a term strictly of American origin. The tall boys first brought into this country from England, probably around 1690, provided the first models for the highboys of the American cabinetmakers. They had flat tops and used six legs—four in front and two at back—

joined by flat but curved stretchers along the front and sides and a flat stretcher in the back. The bottom of the apron below the drawer (or drawers) in front was customarily shaped in designs that followed along the lines of the convex and concave cyma curve. The first highboys had a single wide bottom drawer; some made a bit later had three small drawers at the bottom. Also, some had one wide drawer across the top and others (probably later ones) had two or three across the top.

This general style of history was used in this country through the second decade of the 18th century, supplanted then by those with legs in the Queen Anne style.

In general design. the lowboy followed the style of the highboy stand (or bottom), the earliest having six legs and later ones only four. They had three drawers across the front and legs with inverted cup or trumpet-type turnings and ball feet.

Various types of chairs were made during the William and Mary influence in this country. The Oriental influence was evidenced in high-back cane chairs, some sumptuous ones with a pierced cresting. There also were bannister-backs (which substituted spindles for the caned backs), and the "Boston" type, with a leather seat and back and legs terminating in either Spanish or button feet. Also making its appearance was the "easy chair," now known as the wing chair, with short legs of rudimentary cabriole form in front and of square section in the back. And there appeared corner chairs, often called "roundabouts." These had a curved rail at the back, an open front, one front leg and three additional ones to support the curved back and arms.

There were many changes in chests and the adoption here as in England of veneered drawer fronts and turnip feet. Coming into use just before the end of the century were upright desks with sloping tops, simplest of which was the desk on a frame. The frame consisted of turned legs with turned stretchers and shaped skirt, and the desk proper was a long box with slanting lid and an arrangement of pigeon holes inside. More elaborate was the frame with a chest of drawers on feet, above which was another section containing a writing surface, which was pulled forward and downward to open. The secretary-desk had a full-front surface for writing and the upper section was a fairly tall cabinet containing numerous drawers and pigeon holes with the bottom section containing full-sized drawers.

Some press cupboards continued to be used during the William and Mary period, but there also appeared both moveable and built-in cupboards of pine. For storage and display, there was the pine dresser—a tall frame that often reached close to the ceiling with an enclosed base, sometimes with drawers, and with open shelves above.

The gateleg remained the most popular type of table, and various versions were produced. Though walnut was used abun-

dantly for tables, pine, cherry, maple and other local woods
were substituted in areas of this country in which these woods
were plentiful. Stretcher and dressing tables were produced in
some quantity. Beds changed radically with tall bedsteads coming
in. Some bedstead posts were 15 or more feet high. Posts were
slender and simple—round or octagonal, some decorated with
fluting. About the turn of the century day beds were made
with bannister-type slats instead of cane in their backs and with
ball feet, and cushions were used on the rush seats.

Meanwhile, France had acquired great power and wealth,
which, allied to a native flair for the feminine, enabled her to
excel in the production of fine furniture. Louis XIV provided
his people and his artists with that indispensable lever of great
art, a patron. Not only did he buy what was made, but he
established heavily-subsidized manufactories for the making, under
the guiding control of the central Manufacture des Gobelins,
headed by the noted painter Le Brun. These manufactories produced the magnificent carved gilded furniture, fine tapestries,
porcelains, glass and curios that provided the great new palace
at Versailles with an interior lavishness not known since the days
of the Byzantines and which laved the aristocracy in luxury
and splendor and trouble, and percolated slowly to more bar-
barous parts of civilization via ambassadors and stately visitors.

Afterwards, the better period of Louis XVI was ushered in
with a return to clean lines and an avoidance of unnecessary
decoration. Slender chair legs and the use of gold paint on
woodwork (or even white paint), with pastel shades in fabric
coverings, characterized what was to become, for foreigners, the
most typical of French furniture. The period was influenced
strongly by excavations at Pompeii and Herculaneum, which
suggested classical ornamentation instead of the overdone rococo.
The straining rail disappeared from chairs, and the loose cushion
appeared. Tapestries of the manufactories of the Gobelins, Au-
busson and Beauvais vied with Utrecht velvets striped and pat-
terned to produce, in particular, some of the loveliest chairs
known to man. Magnificent commodes, bureaux and cabinets
were made during the period, but, as in England of the 18th
century, the chair appeared to be the principal item of furniture,
judging from the attention levied upon it, and possibly proceeding
from the fact that this was essentially the polite and social era.

This matter of chairs is so important that a brief recapitula-
tion of highlights of English chair-making from the Carolean
period onwards will help maintain the perspective of it. These
highlights will also reflect those of chair-making in America
since American craftsmen and designers generally followed the
English styles with the onset of new stylistic features in this
country following their introduction in England by a short period
of time.

The typical chair of Charles II has canework in the back and a cane or rush seat. Backs were long and straight; slats were pierced and carved, most frequently with acanthus leafage; rails atop and bottoms of the backs were similarily decorated. The cane or rush original seats have since been replaced, often by a board. Uprights of the backs, legs and rails were of twisted turned work, which, coming into favor a little before the middle of the 17th century, neatly dates the Carolean period chair.

In the period of James II, chairs remained elongated at the backs and heavy in appearance, but the twisted and turned work was not employed so frequently, and there was an increasing tendency to upholster back panels and seats with velvet fastened down by brass-studded nails, showing the influence of Louis XIV furniture.

The chairs of William and Mary are transitional in appearance between the Carolean and the Queen Anne styles; that is, they remain fairly upright and severely rectangular, and are often of carved oak.

With the reign of Queen Anne, change come to a head and stabilizes there in a mode derived partly from the English styles just described and partly from the French. With the spotlight still on the all-significant chair, it will be seen that the hitherto severe and rectangular type hitherto favored in England and America has been replaced by one displaying curves in back, legs and seat, with a vase-shaped splat in the back and a stuffed seat covered with fabric. Simultaneously the leg rails are dispensed with, the cabriole leg is firmly established, and burr walnut is employed for veneer. Claw-and-ball have come into favor (another motif derived from China, where it represented the three-clawed foot of the dragon holding the mystic jewel) and continue to be used until the middle of the 18th century. The serpent foot, better known in this country as the snake foot, has also appeared. These are used most frequently for small tripod tables and stands.

Perhaps, however, the outstanding development is the gradual replacement of walnut as the most popular wood by mahogany, which was introduced between 1715 and 1720, and which soon will dominate all other timbers by virtue of its strength against the worm, its large size, uniform grain, durability, and beauty of color.

We hear much today of "Chippendale furniture." What may be said of the designer and cabinetmaker Chippendale (1718-1779) is that he (or his associates and copyists) took the Queen Anne style as just described and refined it. In essentials the Chippendale group produced Queen Anne furniture, but added a wealth of carving and several small improvements of structure such as the square, straight leg (introduced 1740-1750) and the slender straining rail and graceful little brackets where the front legs join the seat. The innovations of carving, which were preeminently the Chippendale touch, included the lightening of the vase-pattern splat by "ribbon" work so that the splats became delicate openwork screens of finely wrought wood, each line of which was no more than half an inch to an inch wide. Meanwhile "Chinoiserie" reached England the usual generation after its appearance on the European continent and became very popular, thanks to the influence of a prominent architect, Sir William Chambers. Chinese patterns were used by the carvers, who also became influenced by the Gothic revival in the middle of the century to carve slats for chairs after the style of pointed arches.

While the Hepplewhite school, which took its name from the designer George Hepplewhite (died 1786), had a leaning toward curved lines, the school of Sheraton, named after the skilled cabinetmaker and author Thomas Sheraton (1751-1806) favored the straightness of traditional English furniture, though still within the framework of the characteristic pattern consolidated by the Chippendale school. The cabriole leg was discarded and replaced entirely by tapering or reeded legs. Sheraton's preference for satinwood and for delicate inlay and painted decoration took him to the opposite extreme from the furniture of Queen Anne, upon which, however, his style was still firmly based.

Not so with the last great English name of the 18th century, Adam. As mentioned in the concise survey of French furniture, the discovery of the buried Roman city of Pompeii in 1748 and subsequently of Herculaneum influenced a return to classical styles of architecture and furniture design. The brothers Adam (Robert, James, John and William), as architects, transmitted the mode to England. They never made furniture as such but produced designs for it which were followed by others. Actually, when we speak of the Adam influence, it is primarily of the influence of Robert, who was the dominating brother of the four. The Adam designs followed the lines of the Roman furniture unearthed and were characterized by severe yet chaste ornamentation on architectural principles. A favorite design was that of the round or oval rosette, rayed; another was the classical vase, be-ribboned. It was Adam also who probably was first to use the anthemion of honeysuckle ornamentation.

The influence of the Adam style extended to all furniture makers of the second half of the 18th century (including Hepplewhite and Sheraton who copied some of the distinctive Adam features in their design books), and culminated in the so-called English Empire period. This was always a foreign influence and ran for a time side by side with the native stream, then petered out.

The furniture of Queen Victoria is still regarded largely as heavy, unlovely, machine-influenced, mahogany, and French-polished. It can be worthy of those adjectives, but at its best displays a solidity of craftsmanship since vanished in a still more debased age, and some of those great mahogany sideboards, dining tables, yes, and even some of those massive horse-hair sofas will eventually be darling pieces of the collector, who by then will have been able to see in perspective a distinct style of the period.

In America, these various major English designs of which we have been speaking were often closely followed and became the fashion here a few years after they had become popular in England. This was only natural, since the early settlers in this country were, with the exception of a small group of Dutch emigrants, British themselves. There were, however, a number of individualistic and highly-talented American craftsmen who added touches of their own to the English styles, and it is these special touches that now enable us with increasing frequency and accuracy to attribute articles of furniture to particular American cabinetmakers or at least to specific geographical localities.

In this country, widespread adoption of the Queen Anne style began began about 1720 to 1725, but for a good many years, numerous American cabinetmakers adopted certain characteristics of the Queen Anne style and eschewed others. Many of our chairs, for example, were made with the bow back but with earlier legs ending in Spanish feet instead of the cabriole leg, even though in England the cabriole leg was earlier than the bow back.

The finest Chippendale style furniture in America is generally conceded to have been made in the Philadelphia area, where there was a great concentration of wealth and social prestige. The widespread production of this type of furniture began around 1760, half a dozen years after Chippendale's famous and influential book of designs, *The Gentleman and Cabinet-Maker's Director* (to use its short title), was first published. Philadelphia Chippendale follows English Chippendale with considerable faithfulness but did vary in certain minor details. This is not the place to enter upon a discussion of these characteristics which help distinguish American from English-made furniture, but the dealer who wants to know these differences will find several of the books listed in out Selected Bibliography at the end of this volume of great help. Among the great names in Philadelphia cabinetmaking one most often hears those of Thomas Affleck, James Gillingham, John Folwell, Joseph Deleveau, and Edward James.

In other areas of the country names of distinguished cabinetmakers of the 18th century include John Goddard and Job Townsend, Samuel McIntyre, and Duncan Phyfe, to name only three. Many of the outstanding early American cabinetmakers are discussed with authority in Thomas H. Ormsbee's book *Early American Furniture Makers* and in other works, which the reader also will find in our bibliography.

Certainly the best-known name in American furniture of the colonial period is that of Duncan Phyfe, who came to this country from Scotland and developed an astonishingly large business in New York City. Phyfe worked from around 1790 in New York until 1847 but it cannot be said accurately that there is a Duncan Phyfe "style" of furniture in the same sense that there were Queen Anne styles, Chippendale styles, and so on, because Phyfe largely followed the English styles popular in his time, largely the Sheraton, and also the Directory, and the Empire. His greatest contributions were in furniture of the Sheraton style to which he added his own special touches and innovations that lent grace and admirable proportion. We now associate with his work such decorative ornamentation as the urn, the lyre, rosettes, and the water leaf.

Our cabinetmakers turned to the Empire style during the first decade of the 19th century and continued producing pieces based somewhat on English and French models for almost four decades until the Victorian styles took over. Some of Duncan Phyfe's work was in this style as noted above. Many American families also imported Empire pieces from France, and some of these have been coming onto the market lately. But whereas the French Empire craftsmen utilized such decorative designs as sphinxes and military paraphernalia, the Americans substituted instead such designs as the American eagle, the cornucopia, and fruits and floral arrangements.

American Empire pieces made after about 1830 were generally heavy and ponderous and lacking in character with little to commend them except good workmanship and excellent mahogany wood.

Until the past two or three years, the majority of connoisseurs have condemned Victorian furniture *in toto*. Now, however, there seems to be just awakening in this country, whose antiques do not date back nearly so far as do those of most other countries of the world, a realization that fine craftsmanship did prevail during the Victorian period, and that a larger number of Victorian objects than had heretofore been suspected can be adapted to attractive use in modern homes. Early Victorian furniture—that is, articles produced from around 1837 until the middle of the century—are generally considered the most desirable, particularly those that represent first-class workmanship with a minimum of clutter in rosewood or mahogany. Much of the later furniture in walnut was cheapened by the flagrant use of carving and the addition of superfluous ornaments.

Much American Victorian furniture represents adaptations of
earlier styles with the addition of rather crude and inappropriate
details and characteristics. Of the pieces produced in this
country during the Victorian era, a number by John Henry
Belter, a New York cabinetmaker who developed a laminated
wood built up of layers of woods with grains running in opposite
directions, are now attracting attention. These articles are generally in rosewood.

Of interest, now, too, are many quaint and simple pieces
of American country furniture and the simple and unblemished
pieces made by Shaker craftsmen.

Although the dealer who really wants to learn to recognize
American furniture can profit by reading several of the books
listed in our bibliography, we should especially like to command
to the beginner an extremely conscientious and almost exhaustive
study by Edgar G. Miller, *American Antique Furniture,* first
published in1937 and long out of print until it was recently re-
issued in an inexpensive two-volume paperback edition. This
will prove of tremendous value for and interest to the amateur, for
whom it was originally intended.

Finally, we would urge the beginner not to be too concerned
about what appears to be a general confusion—even sometimes
among connoisseurs—relating to periods of furniture and terms
used to describe specific articles of furniture. For example, volumes have been written about "Early American" furniture, and
yet there is confusion as to what period the word "early"
embraces. Are we talking about 17th century furniture? Or both
the 17th and 18th centuries? Wallace Nutting has written about
furniture of the "Pilgrim Century." This covers, roughly, productions from 1620 to 1720.

You will hear the terms "Colonial" furniture, furniture of the
"early Republic," "Federal" furniture, and so on.

Properly used, the reference to "Colonial" furniture should
be to productions of the period preceding the American Revolution. Furniture produced following the Revolutionary War is,
strictly speaking," furniture of the early Republic. More recently,
the two major periods of American furniture production have
been called "Colonial" (embracing styles up to and during the
Revolution) and "Federal" (including styles from 1789 through
the American Empire period).

The confusion, however, becomes more rampant in reference
to certain articles of furniture produced elsewhere than in the
United States and England. In France, the word "fauteuil" is
used to indicate an armchair or elbow chair. A "bergère" is an
easy chair that is upholstered or caned and has low closed sides.
Sometimes, too, the words fauteuil and bergère are used interchangeably. We know what an American bureau is, but in
France the same word describes a writing table or desk. A

"bureau à cylindre" is a French cylinder desk; a "beareau à pente is a slant-front desk; the "bureau plat" is a large writing table with a flat top, and so on.

You will become familiar with all these various terms as time goes on and as you continue to read about furniture and its history. Your primary concern at the outset should be that of knowing whether an article was made in the 17th century or the 19th century; whether it has been extensively repaired and has modern replacements, thereby probably lessening its value; of what wood or woods it is made, and—most of all—whether it is the sort of piece that is in demand and is therefore worth buying in the first place.

Chapter XI

A Final Word

There are more people collecting something today than at any period of history. The opportunities, therefore, have never been greater for success in the business of selling antiques for those who possess the proper attributes, are willing to work hard, and are eager to learn more about collectible objects.

Few great fortunes are made in the antiques business. Those that have been made are the exception, not the rule. But this business can yield a livelihood, even a substantial one, for those willing to play the game properly.

There are still many individuals who buy junk—many because it is cheap, others because they are unable to distinguish junk from objects of merit, and there are undoubtedly a few who buy it simply because junk fascinates them. But if junk fascinates you, then antiques selling is not the business into which you should sink your hard-earned cash today. For the junk buyers today are in the minority. Americans are becoming aware of quality, and that is what they are seeking and what they are willing to pay for.

Under the existing structure of taxation and with inflation continuing despite torturous efforts to halt it, money as such is losing the magic it once possessed. The interest paid on such things as savings accounts in banking institutions is negated by inflation. Stocks are a gamble only for those who have risk capital to spare. But the long history of antiques has been one of an upward climb in value, and the astute investors of the 1970s will turn increasingly to antiques of genuine merit as a sound investment for the long run.

Our standard of taste is rising, too. We are buying antiques not merely as an investment but also because we are learning to appreciate them and because we are learning how to utilize them properly in the decor of our homes and even our offices.

The wise dealer who decides to specialize may not be able, at least at the outset, to buy the best in his chosen field—but he would do well to buy the best he can afford.

The dealer who wants to be successful will also keep intimately abreast of changing tastes and trends. He will read the better antiques periodicals regularly and thoroughly and certainly will not skip the advertisements of articles wanted and for sale, for these, too, are a weather vane for trends.

Something new is being discovered about some antique or category of antiques almost every day, and the earnest researchers who make these discoveries often fashion their findings into books. Half a century ago many antiques dealers could scarcely read or write. Today the dealer without a library of basic and good reference books is lost indeed.

In the field of selling antiques, knowledge is power as never before; and this is no less true in the field of buying. It is not enough to be able to recognize a piece of Belleek: it is necessary to determine whether it is a piece of Irish or of American Belleek and further to know whether it is old or new, since the production of Belleek still flourishes in the isle of the Blarney Stone and the shamrock.

The dealer who has read enough to know will not go into the auction room and bid a substantial sum for a Wedgwood creamware plate that he recognizes as being a 20th century piece. Nor will be overly charmed by 20th century bisque figurines, which pale indeed by comparison with those produced in the 18th and even early 19th centuries. He will know that Meissen productions of the 18th century cannot be come by for a pittance, that there was a severe decline in the quality of Meissen wares in the mid-19th century, and that early 20th century Meissen wares returned to superior quality.

The successful dealer will also keep abreast of reproductions, which have reached such a stage today that they are beginning to constitute a nightmare for collector and dealer alike. Failure of Congress thus far to enact legislation providing for the indelible marking of reproduction antique glassware has dealt a devastating blow to sales of certain types of glass, the reproductions of which are, in some cases, of better quality than the originals. It is the dealer whose knowledge is sufficient to enable him to guarantee a piece to be original who sells glass today. There are still some dealers—alas!—who answer customers' inquiries as to whether a piece is old or new by commenting only, "'Well, I bought it for an old piece."

The standard of education is rising swiftly and to succeed today it is necessary to be learned and knowledgeable beyond the blackest nightmares of our fathers. A good many museums and similar institutions housing antiques are today offering fellowships that provide an opportunity for studying antiques while working, and many aspiring young men and women are making application for and are being granted such fellowships or internships.

Others are preparing themselves in college by taking courses in such studies as archaeology and art appreciation. Still others spend their summer vacations visiting museums of antiques, of which there are an abundance in this country. Those interested in acquiring knowledge in this manner should have available Herbert and Marjorie Katz's book, *Museums, U.S.A.: A History & Guide,* which lists more than 2,500 museums, cross-indexed and arranged according to city and state.

Just being launched in this country is a series of tours of the antiques capitals of what we quaintly refer to as the "Old World." Participation in such a tour guided by experts can be well worth while, and costs generally are below those of individual trips abroad.

As the older antiques disappear increasingly into museums and the private collections of the very wealthy or are destroyed by the certain ravages of time, the focal point of collectors moves from earlier to more recent centuries, and the definition of what is antique is ever moving forward in time. Some years hence the novel plastic furniture, the television sets, and the cigarette lighters of today will have the same fascination for collectors as 18th century wine-coolers, calling card stands, and Sandwich glass hold for us at the present.

There will aways be an antiques trade so long as there are men and women who like to possess fascinating and beautiful articles of the past.

The coming gold mine is unquestionably the Victorian period, pronouncements of the "experts" to the contrary notwithstanding. The depths of this period have scarcely been plumbed as yet. Veteran dealers tell us they remember having seen in old homes and business establishments really exquisite chairs, tables, and small Victorian pieces they could have picked up for a pittance just a few years ago if they had possessed the foreknowledge they should have had. But thousands of these products of the Victorian period are still available for what certainly will seem like a pittance a few years hence.

Here is a field, of course, in which the dealer must exercise discrimination, acquiring cheaply when he can articles of solid merit and interest and eschewing those that on their face are little more than monstrous. And still we must remember that tastes and standards of beauty change and that our children and grandchildren may look upon the Tiffany glass we currently adore as something perfectly atrocious.

We must remember that as a civilized nation, the United States is still in its infancy when compared to Rome and Greece or Egypt or many other countries of this world. The only tombs from which we have extracted treasures of perhaps eons past are the burial tombs of the American Indians, and while many of these artifacts are of great interest, they may not compare in value with the treasures that have been extracted from the tombs of the ancient Pharoahs. Articles fashioned on our shores, excluding those made by our red-skinned predecessors, date back only to the 17th century and most objects from that century are now quite scarce. So if we collect Americana, we must concentrate largely on articles produced from the 18th century onwards. We do have our own antiques but we do not have our own antiquities.

At this point we would venture the opinion, if we dared, that some of us are prone to lavish an excess of veneration on age alone—as if age were the sole or even the major criterion of intrinsic merit or extrinsic worth. The lamentable fact—lamentable for those who have attained the age that your authors have—seems to be that it is youthfulness and not age that merits honor today. We are told that those who have passed the age of 30 are mistrusted; that those who have passed the age of 40 are outmoded; and that those who have passed the age of 50 might as well die—were it not for the high cost of dying.

One opinion we do dare reiterate is that some of our early 19th century and even later 19th century productions are eminently worth salvaging and preserving and even treasuring. They are not all antiques, but they are becoming collectible objects, and they provide the storehouse of minor treasures for which a rapidly increasing percentage of our populace is now beginning to clamor. This serves to point up the fact that an addiction to collecting—even if it's only money or testimonials to our splendid character—is becoming a phenomenon of our times.

So while we doubt that we should worship the past, we do think we should know something about it so that we can appreciate it and perhaps even learn from it some of the reasons for our own behavior today. We may discover that our great-grandparents were not necessarily the stuffy individuals we had assumed them to be and that they, too, found life full of delight and fascination.

And those who aspire to become dealers in this ever-broadening field of antiques, should also know that many of the 19th century objects, which some of us may even remember with a pleasant nostalgia, do constitute for our younger generation the artifacts of an era that is singularly remote and marvelously quaint. The spacecraft and the computer may be commonplace to the young men and women now emerging bright-eyed and hopefully from our colleges and universities, but buttonhooks and Rose O'Neill's Kewpies are for them the creations of a civilization as strange as that which flourished during those days in which the lions fed blissfully upon a diet of Christians.

We suggest there should be preserved our interesting, if not immensely valuable, creations of the 19th century while we still have available the basic materials for research about their background. It would be a deplorable state of affairs if our future historians mistook our opalescent Sandwich glass curtain tie-backs for oversized earrings worn by an earlier generation of of American Amazons or identified our 19th century apple corers as generators of electrical impulses.

We should like to conclude this final chapter with a few words of thanks to the many collectors and dealers who have given us advice and help with particular thanks to Mr. James H. Futch, CPA, of Atlanta, for his assistance with the chapter on taxes.

Selected Bibliography

The majority of these books are still in print and may be obtained from or ordered through your book store, or, in cases of books privately published, direct from the authors. Others will be found in public libraries or may be obtained from dealers in out-of-print books.

GENERAL BOOKS ON ANTIQUES

BUTLER, Joseph T. *American Antiques, 1800-1900*. The Odyssey Press, New York City.

COLE, Ann Kilborn. *How to Collect the "New" Antiques*. David McKay Company, New York City.

COMSTOCK, Helen (Ed.). *The Concise Encyclopedia of American Antiques*. Hawthorne Books, Inc., New York City.

COWIE, Donald. *How to Identify and Collect Antiques*. A. S. Barnes & Co., Inc., Cranbury, New Jersey.

COWIE, Donald & Keith Henshaw. *Antique Collector's Dictionary*. Arco Books, Inc., New York City.

DREPPARD, Carl W. *A Dictionary of American Antiques*. Award Books, New York City.

————— & Marjorie Mathews Smith. *Handbook of Tomorrow's Antiques*. Thomas Y. Crowell Company, New York City.

JENKINS, Dorothy. *A Fortune in the Junk Pile*. Crown Publishers, Inc., New York City.

KOVEL, Ralph and Terry. *Know Your Antiques*. Crown Publishers, Inc., New York City.

McCLINTON, Katharine Morrison. *Antique Collecting*. Fawcett Books, Greenwich, Connecticut.

————— *The Complete Book of American Country Antiques*. Coward-McCann, Inc., New York City.

————— *The Complete Book of Small Antiques Collecting*. Coward-McCann, Inc., New York City.

MEBANE, John. *New Horizons in Collecting: Cinderella Antiques*. A. S. Barnes & Company, Cranbury, N.J.

————— *The Poor Man's Guide to Antique Collecting*. Doubleday & Company, Inc., Garden City, N.Y.

————— *What's New That's Old: Offbeat Collectibles*. A. S. Barnes & Company, Cranbury, N.J.

MICHAEL, George. *George Michael's Treasury of Federal Antiques*. Hawthorne Books, Inc., New York City.

WINCHESTER, Alice. *How to Know American Antiques*. The New American Library, New York City.

CERAMICS

ATLMAN, Seymour and Violet. *The Book of Buffalo Pottery.* Crown Publishers, Inc., New York City.

BARRET, Richard Carter. *Bennington Pottery and Porcelain.* Bonanza Books, New York City.

EBERLEIN, Harold Donaldson and Roger Wearne Ramsdell. *The Practical Book of Chinaware.* Halcyon House, New York City.

GODDEN, Geoffrey A. *British Pottery and Porcelain, 1780-1850.* A. S. Barnes & Company, Inc., Cranbury, New Jersey.

—— *British Pottery and Porcelain: An Illustrated Encyclopedia of Marked Specimens.* Crown Publishers, Inc., New York City.

HAGGAR, Reginald G. *The Concise Encyclopedia of Continental Pottery and Porcelain.* Hawthorne Books, Inc., New York City.

HENZKE, Lucile. *American Art Pottery.* Thomas Nelson, Inc., Camden, N.J.

HUGHES, Bernard and Therle. *The Collector's Encyclopedia of English Ceramics.* Abbey Library, London.

—— & —— *English Porcelain and Bone China, 1743-1850.* Frederick A. Praeger, Publishers, New York City.

HUGHES, G. Bernard. *English Pottery and Porcelain Figures.* Frederick A. Praeger, Publishers, New York City.

IMBER, Diana. *Collecting European Delft and Faience.* Frederick A. Praeger, Publishers, New York City.

PECK, Herbert. *The Book of Rookwood Pottery.* Crown Publishers, Inc., New York City.

PENKALA, Marie. *European Porcelain.* Charles E. Tuttle Company, Rutland, Vermont.

—— *Europeana Pottery.* Charles E. Tuttle Company, Rutland, Vermont.

LANDAIS, Hubert. *French Porcelain.* G. P. Putnam's Sons, New York City.

PURVIANCE, Louise and Evan & Norris F. Schneider. *Zanesville Art Pottery in Color.* Mid-America Book Company, Leon, Iowa.

RAMSAY, John. *American Potters and Pottery.* Tudor Publishing Company, New York City.

SAVAGE, George. *Ceramics for the Collector.* Rockliff, London.

—— *Porcelain through the Ages.* Penguin Books, Inc., Baltimore, Maryland.

SCHWARTZ, Marvin D. *A Collector's Guide to Antique American Ceramics.* Doubleday & Company, Inc., Garden City, N.Y.

WARE, George W. *German and Austrian Porcelain.* Bonanza Books, New York City.

SPARGO, John. *Early American Pottery and China.* The Century Company, New York City.

GLASS

AVILA, George C. *The Pairpoint Story.* Privately Published, Mattapoisset, Massachusetts.

BARRET, Richard Carter. *Blown and Pressed American Glass.* Forward Color Productions, Inc., Manchester, Vermont.

BELKNAP, E. M. *Milk Glass.* Crown Publishers, Inc., New York City.

BLOUNT, Berniece and Henry. *French Cameo Glass.* Privately Published, Des Moines, Iowa.

BRAHMER, Bonnie J. *Custard Glass.* Privately Published, Springfield, Missouri.

CROMPTON, Sidney (Ed.). *English Glass.* Hawthorne Books, Inc., New York City.

DANIEL, Dorothy. *Cut and Engraved Glass.* M. Barrows & Company, New York City.

DAVIS, Derek C. & Keith Middlemas. Colored Glass. Clarkson N. Potter, Inc., New York City.

DREPPARD, Carl W. *The ABC's of Old Glass.* Doubleday & Company, Inc., Garden City, N.Y.

ERICSON, Eric S. *A Guide to Colored Steuben Glass, 1903-1933.* (Also Book Two). Privately Published, Denver, Colorado.

GROVER, Ray and Lee. Art Glass Nouveau. Charles E. Tuttle Company, Rutland, Vermont.

HARTUNG, Marion T. *Carnival Glass.* (8 books in this series.) Privately Published, Emporia, Kansas.

HAYNES, E. Barrington. Glass through the Ages. Penguin Books, Inc., Baltimore, Maryland.

HERRICK, Ruth. *Greentown Glass.* Privately Published, Lowell, Michigan.

HOTCHKISS, John F. *Carder's Steuben Glass.* Privately published, Rochester, New York.

HUGHES, G. Bernard. *English Glass for the Collector, 1660-1860.* Praeger Publishers, New York City.

HUNTER, Frederick William. *Stiegel Glass.* Dover Publications, Inc., New York City.

KAMM, Minnie Watson. *Minnie Kamm Watson's Pitcher Books.* Edited by Serry Wood. Century House, Watkins Glen, N.Y.

KNITTLE, Rhea Mansfield, *American Glass.* The Century Company, New York City.

KOCH, Robert. *Louis C. Tiffany, Rebel in Glass.* Crown Publishers, Inc., New York City.

LAGERBERG, Ted and Vi. *A Color Picture Guide to 100 Types of Collectible Glass.* Modern Photographers, New Port Richey, Florida.

——— & ——— *A Color Guide to Collectible Glass* (Books 2, 3 and 4). Modern Photographers, New Port Richey, Florida.

LEE, Ruth Webb. *Early American Pressed Glass.* Privately Published, Wellesley Hills, Massachusetts.

——— *Sandwich Glass.* Privately Published, Wellesley Hills, Massachusetts.

———— *Victorian Glass.* Privately Published, Wellesley Hills, Massachusetts.

———— & James H. Rose. *American Glass Cup Plates.* Privately Published, Northborough, Massachusetts.

LINDSEY, Bessie M. *American Historical Glass.* Chalres E. Tuttle Company, Rutland, Vermont.

McKEARIN, Geo. S. and Helen. *American Glass.* Crown Publishers, Inc., New York City.

———— & ———— *Two Hundred Years of American Blown Glass.* Crown Publishers, Inc., New York City.

METZ, Alice Hulett. *Early American Pattern Glass.* Privately Published, Chicago.

———— *Much More Early American Pattern Glass.* Privately Published, Chicago.

MOORE, N. Hudson. *Old Glass, European and American.* Tudor Publishing Company, New York City.

NORTHEND, Mary Harrod. *American Glass.* Dodd, Mead Company, New York City.

PEARSON, J. Michael and Dorothy T. *American Cut Glass for the Discriminating Collector.* Privately Published, Miami Beach, Florida.

———— & ———— *A Study of American Cut Glass Collections.* Privately Published, Miami Beach, Florida.

PETERSON, Arthur G. *400 Trademarks on Glass.* Washington College Press, Takoma Park, Maryland.

PRESZNICK, Rose M. *Carnival and Iridescent Glass.* (4 books in the series.) Privately Published, Lodi, Ohio.

REVI, Albert Christian. *American Art Nouveau Glass.* Thomas Nelson & Sons, Camden, New Jersey.

———— *American Cut and Engraved Glass.* Thomas Nelson & Sons, Camden, New Jersey.

———— *American Pressed Glass and Figure Bottles.* Thomas Nelson & Sons, Camden, New Jersey.

———— *Nineteenth Century Glass: Its Genesis and Development.* Thomas Nelson & Sons, Camden, New Jersey.

ROSE, James H. *The Story of American Pressed Glass of the Lacy Period.* Corning Museum of Glass, Corning, New York.

SCHWARTZ, Marvin D. *Collectors' Guide to Antique American Glass.* Doubleday & Company, Inc., Garden City, New York.

WATKINS, Lura Woodside. *Cambridge Glass, 1818 to 1888. The story of the New England Glass Company.* Bramhall House, New York City.

WHITLOW, Harry H. *Art, Colored & Cameo Glass.* Privately Published, Riverview, Michigan.

WILLS, Geoffrey. *English and Irish Glass.* Doubleday & Company, Inc., Garden City, New York.

FURNITURE

ANDREWS, Edward Deming and Faith. *Religion in Wood. A Book of Shaker Furniture.* Indiana University Press, Bloomington, Indiana.

———— & ———— *Shaker Furniutre.* Dover Publications, Inc., New York City.

ARONSON, Joseph. *The Encyclopedia of Furniture.* Crown Publishers, Inc., New York City.

BOGER, Louise Ade. *The Complete Guide to Furniture Styles.* Charles Scribner's Sons, New York City.

———— *Furniture Past & Present.* Doubleday & Company, Garden City, New York.

CESCINSKY, Herbert. *English Furniture from Gothic to Sheraton.* Dover Publishers, Inc., New York City.

———— *The Gentle Art of Faking Furniture.* Dover Publications, Inc., New York City.

———— and George Leland Hunter. *English and American Furniture.* Garden City Publishing Company, Garden City, New York.

DOWNS, Joseph. *American Furniture: Queene Anne and Chippendale Periods in The Henry Francis duPont Winterthur Museum.* Viking Press, New York City.

EDWARDS, Ralph and Margaret Jourdain. *Georgian Cabinet Makers.* Country Life, Ltd., London.

GLOAG, John. *A Short Dictionary of Furniture.* Holt, Rinehart & Winston, New York City.

GRANDJEAN, Serge. *Empire Furniture, 1800-1825.* Taplinger Pubishing Company, New York City.

GROTZ, George. *Antiques You Can Decorate With.* Doubleday & Company, Inc., New York City.

———— *The New Antiques: Knowing and Buying Victorian Furniture.* Doubleday & Company, Inc., New York City.

———— *The New Antiques: Knowing and Buying Victorian Furniture.* Doubleday & Company, Inc., New York City.

HAYWARD, Helena (Ed.). *World Furniture, An Illustrated History.* McGraw-Hill Book Company, New York City.

HINCKLEY, F. Lewis. *A Directory of Antique French Furniture.* Crown Publshiers, Inc., New York City.

———— *A Directory of Antique Furniture.* Bonanza Books, New York City.

HUGHES, Therle. *Old English Furniture.* Frederick A. Praeger, Publishers, New York City.

KOVEL, Ralph and Terry. *American County Furniture, 1780-1875.* Crown Publishers, Inc., New York City.

LOCKWOOD, Luke Vincent. Colonial Furniture in America. Castle Books, New York City.

McCLINTON, Katharine Morrison. *An Outline of Period Furniture.* Charles Scribner's Sons, New York City.

MILLER, Edgar G. *American Antique Furniture*. (Two volumes). Dover Publications, Inc., New York City.

MONTGOMERY, Charles F. *American Furniture, the Federal Period, in the Henry Francis duPont Winterthur Museum*. The Viking Press, New York City.

MORNINGSTAR, Connie. *Flapper Furniture*. Wallace-Homestead Book Co., Des Moines, Iowa.

NUTTING, Wallace. *American Windsors, a Windsor Handbook*. Old America Company, Framingham, Massachusetts, and Boston. (A reprint is available in paperback from Cracker Barrel Press, Southampton, N.Y.)

———— *Furniture of the Pilgrim Century*. (Two volumes). Dover Publications, Inc., New York City.

ORMSBEE, Thomas H(amilton). *Early American Furniture Makers*. Archer House, New York City.

———— *Field Guide to American Victorian Furniture*. Bonanza Books, New York City.

———— *Field Guide to Early American Furniture*. Little, Brown & Company, Boston.

———— *The Story of American Furniture*. Pyramid Books, New York City.

OTTO, Celia Jackson. *American Furniture of the Nineteeenth Century*. The Viking Press, New York City.

ROGERS, John C. *English Furniture*. (Revised & Enlarged by Margaret Jourdain.) Country Life, Ltd., London.

SACK, Albert. *Fine Points of Furniture: Early American*. Crown Publishers, Inc., New York City.

SYMONDS, R. W. and B. B. Whineray. *Victorian Furniture*. Country Life, Ltd., London.

WILLIAMS, H. Lionel. *Country Furniture of Early America*. A. S. Barnes & Company, Inc., Cranbury, New Jersey.

VICTORIAN ANTIQUES

BENTLEY, Nicholas. *The Victorian Scene: 1837-1901*. Weidenfeld & Nicolson, London. Distributed by the New York Graphic Society, Greenwich, Connecticut.

DREPPARD, Carl W. *Victorian, the Cinderella of Antiques*. Doubledays & Company, Garden City, New York.

GLOAG, John. *Victorian Comfort. A Social History of Design from 1830-1900*. Adam and Charles Black, London.

BALSTON, Thomas. *Staffordshire Portarit Figures of the Victorian Age*. Faber & Faber, London.

HUGHES, G. Bernard. *Victorian Pottery & Porcelain*. Country Life, Ltd., London.

LICHTEN, Frances. *Decorative Art of Victoria's Era*. Charles Scribner's Sons, New York City.

McCLINTON, Katharine Morrison. *Collecting American Victorian Antiques.* Charles Scribner's Sons, New York City.

MAAS, John. *The Gingerbread Age. A View of Victorian America.* Bramhall House, New York City.

PETER, Mary. *Collecting Victoriana.* Praeger Publishers, New York City.

REYNOLDS, Ernest. *Collecting Victorian Porcelain.* Praeger Publishers, New York City.

SHULL, Thelma. *Victorian Antiques.* Charles E. Tuttle Company, Rutland, Vermont.

WOOD, Violet. *Victoriana. A Collector's Guide.* G. Bell and Sons, London.

SILVER AND SILVER PLATE & OTHER METALS

BELL, Malcolm. *Old Pewter.* George Newnes, Ltd., London.

BURGESS, Fred W. *Chats on Old Copper and Brass.* T. Fisher Unwin, London.

BURTON, E. Milby. *South Carolina Silversmiths, 1690-1860.* Charles E. Tuttle Company, Rutland, Vermont.

CARRE, Louis. *A Guide to Old French Plate.* Charles Scribner's Sons, New York City.

CRIPPS, Wilfred Joseph. *Old English Plate, Ecclesiastical, Decorative, and Domestic; Its Makers and Marks.* John Murray, London.

DELIEB, Eric. *Investing in Silver.* Clarkson N. Potter, Inc., New York City.

———— *Silver Boxes.* Clarkson N. Potter, Inc., New York City.

ENSKO, Stephen G. C. *American Silversmiths and Their Marks.* Cracker Barrel Press, Southampton, New York.

FALES, Martha Candy. *Early American Silver.* Funk & Wagnalls, New York City.

GOULD, Mary Earle. *Antique Tin and Tole Ware: Its History and Romance.* Charles E. Tuttle Company, Rutland, Vermont.

HAYDEN, Arthur. *Chats on Old Silver.* Revised & Edited by Cyril G. E. Bunt. Ernest Benn, Limited, London.

HOOD, Graham. *American Silver.* Praeger Publishers, New York City.

HUGHES, Bernard and Therle. *Three Centuries of English Domestic Silver, 1500-1820.* Frederick A. Praeger, Publishers, New York City.

JACKSON, Sir Charles James. *English Goldsmiths and Their Marks.* Dover Publications, Inc., New York City.

JACOBS, Carl. *Guide to American Pewter.* Robert M. McBride Company, New York City.

KAUFFMAN, Henry J. *American Copper & Brass.* Thomas Nelson & Sons, Camden, New Jersey.

———— *Early American Ironware.* Charles E. Tuttle Company, Rutland, Vermont.

LINDSAY, J. Seymour. *Iron and Brass Implements of the English and American House.* Alec Tiranti, London. (Distributed by Herman Publishing Service, Stamford, Connecticut.)

McCLINTON, Katharine Morrison. *Collecting American Nineteenth Century Silver.* Charles Scribner's Sons, New York City.

MASSE, H. J. L. J. *The Pewter Collector. A Guide to English Pewter with Some Reference to Foreign Work.* Herbert Jenkins, Ltd., London.

MOORE, N. Hudson. *Old Pewter, Brass, Copper & Sheffield Plate.* Charles E. Tuttle Co., Rutland, Vt.

OKIE, Howard Pitcher. *Old Silver and Old Sheffield Plate.* Doubleday, Doran, Garden City, New York.

POWERS, Beatrice Farnsworth and Olive Floyd. *Early American Decorated Tinware.* Hastings House, New York City.

RAINWATER, Dorothy T. (Ed. and Comp.). *American Silver Manufacturers.* Everybodys Press, Hanover, Pennsylvania.

———— and Donna H. Felger. *American Spoons, Souvenir and Historical.* Thomas Nelson & Sons, Camden, New Jersey, and Everybodys Press, Hanover, Pennsylvania.

STOW, Millicent. *American Silver.* Gramercy Publishing Company, New York City.

TAYLOR, Gerald. *Silver.* Penguin Books, Baltimore, Maryland.

WARDLE, Patricia. *Victorian Silver and Silver-plate.* Herbert Jenkins, London.

WILLS, Geoffrey. *Collecting Copper and Brass.* Arco Publications, London.

WYLER, Seymour B. *The Book of Sheffield Plate.* Crown Publishers, Inc., New York City.

BOOKS OF MARKS AND IDENTIFICATION

CHAFFERS, William. *Marks and Monograms on European and Oriental Pottery and Porcelain.* Reeves & Turner, London.

————*Hall-Marks on Gold and Silver Plate.* Reeves & Turner, London.

GODDEN, Geoffrey A. *British Pottery and Porcelain: an Illustrated Encyclopedia of Marked Specimens.* Crown Publishers, Inc., New York City.

———— *The Handbook of British Pottery & Porcelain Marks.* Praeger Publishers, New York City.

GRAHAM, James Jr. *Early American Silver Marks.* Privately Published, New York City.

HARTMAN, Urban. *Porcelain and Pottery Marks.* Privately Published, New York City.

HAGGAR, Reginald G. *The Concise Encyclopedia of Continental Pottery and Porcelain.* Hawthorne Books, Inc., New York City.

KOVEL, Ralph M. and Terry H. *Dictionary of Marks—Pottery and Porcelain.* Crown Publishers, Inc., New York City.

MACDONALD-TAYLOR, Margaret (Ed.). *A Dictionary of Marks. Metalwork, Furniture, Ceramics.* Hawthorne Books, Inc., New York City.

ORMSBEE, Thomas H. *English China and Its Marks.* Channel Press-Deerfield Editions, Ltd., New York City.

THORN, C. Jordan. *The Handbook of American Silver and Pewter Marks.* Tudor Publishing Company, New York City.

———— *Handbook of Old Pottery and Porcelain Marks.* Tudor Publishing Company, New York City.

ART

BARKER, Virgil. *American Painting: History and Interpretation.* Bonanza Books, New York City.

CARRICK, Alice Van Leer. *A History of American Silhouettes: A Collector's Guide—1790-1840.* Charles E. Tuttle Company, Rutland, Vermont.

CHENEY, Sheldon. *A Primer of Modern Art.* Horace Liveright, New York City.

———— *The Story of Modern Art.* The Viking Press, New York City.

CRAVEN, Thomas. *A Tresaury of American Prints.* Simon & Schuster, New York City.

CROUSE, Russell. *Mr. Currier and Mr. Ives.* Doubleday, Doran, Garden City, New York.

DREPPARD, Carl W. *American Pioneer Arts & Artists.* Pond-Ekberg Company, Springfield, Massachusetts.

———— *Early American Prints.* The Century Company, New York City.

EMANUEL, Frank L. *Etching and Etchings. A Guide to Technique and to Print Collecting.* Pitman Publishing Corporation, New York City.

FLEXNER, James Thomas. *America's Old Masters.* Revised edition. Dover Publications, Inc., New York City.

GOMBRICH, E. H. *The Story of Art.* Phaidon Publishers, Inc., New York City.

GROCE, George C. and David H. Wallace. *The New York Historical Society's Dictionary of Artists in America.* Yale University Press, New Haven, Connecticut.

HAGGAR, Reginald C. *A Dictionary of Art Terms.* Hawthorne Books, Inc., New York City.

LONDON, Hannah R. *Miniatures and Silhouettes of Early American Jews.* Charles E. Tuttle Company, Rutland, Vermont.

PETERS, Harry T. *Currier & Ives: Printmakers to the American People.* Doubleday, Doran & Company, Garden City, New York.

PISCHEL, Gina. *A World History of Art.* Golden Press, New York City.

POLLEY, Robert L. (General Ed.). *America's Folk Art*. G. P. Putnam's Sons, New York City, in association with Country Beautiful Foundation.

WILLIAMS, Guy R. *Collecting Pictures*. Frederick A. Praeger, Publishers, New York City.

ORIENTAL ANTIQUES

BEURDELEY, Michael. *The Chinese Collector through the Centuries*. Charles E. Tuttle Company, Rutland, Vermont.

BOGER, H. Batterson. *The Traditional Arts of Japan*. Bonanza Books, New York City.

BURLING, Judith. *Chinese Art*. Bonanza Books, New York City.

BUSHELL, Raymond. *The Wonderful World of Netsuke*. Charles E. Tuttle Company, Rutland, Vermont.

CAMMANN, SCHUYLER. *Substance and Symbol in Chinese Toggles*. University of Pennsylvania Press, Philadelphia.

COX, Warren E. *Chinese Ivory Sculpture*. Bonanza Books, New York City.

DU BOULAY, Anthony. *Chinese Porcelain*. C. P. Putnam's Sons, New York City.

FICKE, Arthur Davison. *Chats on Japanese Prints*. Frederick A. Stokes Company, New York City.

GOMPERTZ, G. St. G. M. *Celadon Wares*. Praeger Publishers, New York City.

HAYASHIYA, Seizo and Gakuji Hasebe. *Chinese Ceramics*. Charles E. Tuttle Company, Rutland, Vermont.

HOBSON, R. L. *Chinese Art*. Springs Books, London.

―――― & E. A. Morse. *Chinese, Corean and Japanese Potteries*. Japan Society.

JOHNES, Raymond. *Japanese Art*. Spring Books, London.

MACKENZIE, Finlay. *Chinese Art*. Spring Books, London.

MUDGE, Jean McClure. *Chinese Export Porcelain for the American Trade, 1785-1835*. University of Delaware Press. Distributed by University Publishers, Inc., New York City.)

NEWMAN, Alex R. and Egerton Ryerson. *Japanese Art*. A. S. Barnes & Company, Cranbury, New Jersey.

PALMER, J. P. *Jade*. Spring Books, London.

PRODAN, Mario. *An Introduction to Chinese Art*. Spring Books, London.

SANDERS, Herbert S. *The World of Japanese Ceramics*. Kodansha International, Ltd., Palo Alto, California.

TURK, F. A. *Japanese Objects d'Art*. Arco Publications, London.

WILLS, Geoffrey. *Ivory*. A. S. Barnes & Company, Inc., Cranbury, New Jersey.

CARPETS, RUGS & OTHER TEXTILES

BAKER, Muriel L. *A Handbook of American Crewel Embroidery*. Charles E. Tuttle Company, Rutland, Vermont.

BAKER, Wilma Sinclair LeVan. *The Silk Pictures of Thomas Stevens*. Exposition Press, New York City.

CANDEE, Helen Churchill. *The Tapestry Book*. Tudor Publishing Company, New York City.

DE CALATCHI, Robert. *Oriental Carpets*. Charles E. Tuttle Company, Rutland, Vermont.

FINLEY, Ruth E. *Old Patchwork Quilts and the Women Who Made Them*. J. B. Lippincott Company, Philadelphia.

HALL, Eliza Calvert. *A Book of Hand-Woven Coverlets*. Charles E. Tuttle Company, Rutland, Vermont.

ICKIS, Marguerite. *The Standard Book of Quilt Making and Collecting*. Dover Publications, Inc., New York City.

JACOBSEN, Charles W. *Check Points on How to Buy Oriental Rugs*. Charles E. Tuttle Company, Rutland, Vermont.

LOWES, Mrs. Emily L. *Chats on Old Lace and Needlework*. T. Fisher Unwin, London.

MOORE, N. Hudson. *The Lace Book*. Frederick A. Stokes Company, New York City.

RIES, Estelle H. *American Rugs*. World Publishing Company, Cleveland, Ohio.

TURKHAN, Kudret H. *Islamic Rugs*. Frederick A. Praeger, Publishers, New York City.

WAUGH, Elizabeth and Edith Foley. *Collecting Hooked Rugs*. The Century Company, New York City.

WEEKS, Jeanne G. and Donald Treganowan. *Rugs and Carpets of Europe and the Western World*.

MISCELLANEOUS SPECIALTIES

CLOCKS & WATCHES

BAILLIE, G. H., C. Clutton and C. A. Ilbert. *Britain's Old Clocks and Watches and Their Makers*. (Seventh Edition.) Bonanza Books, New York City.

BRUTON, Eric. *Dictionary of Clocks and Watches*. Archer House, New York City.

CLUTTON, Cecil and George Daniels. *Watches*. The Viking Press, New York City.

CUMHAILL, P. W. *Investing in Clocks and Watches*. Clarkson N. Potter, New York City.

ECKHARDT, George H. *Pennsylvania Clocks and Clockmakers*. Bonanza Books, New York City.

JOHNSON, Chester. *Clocks and Watches*. Odyssey Press, New York City.

LLOYD, H. Alan. *Chats on Old Clocks*. A. A. Wyn, New York City.
———— *The Complete Book of Old Clocks*. G. P. Putnam's Sons, New York City.

PALMER, Brooks. *Book of American Clocks*. The Macmillan Company, New York City.

TYLER, E. J. *European Clocks.* Frederick A. Praeger, Publishers, New York City.

WENHAM, Edward. *Old Clocks.* Spring Books, London.

DOLLS

ANGIONE, Genevieve. *All-Bisque and Half-Bisque Dolls.* Thomas Nelson, & Sons, Camden, New Jersey.

FAWCETT, Clara. *Dolls—A Guide to Collecting.* Century House, Watkins Glen, New York.

JACOBS, Flora Gill and Estrid Faurholt. *A Book of Dolls and Dolls Houses.* Charles E. Tuttle Company, Rutland, Vermont.

JOHL, Janet Pagter. *The Fascinating Story of Dolls.* H. L. Lindquist, New York City.

ST. GEORGE, Eleanor. *Dolls of Three Centuries.* Charles Scribner's Sons, New York City.

——— The Dolls of Yesterday. Charles Scribner's Sons, New York City.

JEWELRY

BAERWALD, Marcus and Tom Mahoney. *Gems and Jewelry Today. An Account of the Romance and Values of Gems, Jewelry, Watches and Silverware.* Marcel Rodd Company, New York City.

BRADFORD, Ernle. *English Victorian Jewellery.* Spring Books, London.

DARLING, Ada. *Antique Jewelry Identification with Price Guide.* Mid-America Book Company. Leon, Iowa.

FALKINER, Richard. *Investing in Antique Jewelry.* Clarkson N. Potter, Inc., New York City.

LIGHTING DEVICES

FREEMAN, Larry. *New Light on Old Lamps.* (Revised edition.) Century House, Watkins Glen, New York.

HAYWARD, Arthur H. *Colonial Lighting.* Dover Publications, Inc., New York City.

MILITARY ITEMS

ANDERSON, L. J. *Japanese Armour.* Stackpole Books, Harrisburg, Pennsylvania.

CARMAN, W. Y. *British Military Uniforms form Contemporary Pictures.* Arco Publishing Company, Inc., New York City.

LATHAM, R. J. Wilkinson. *British Military Bayonets from 1700 to 1945.* Arco Publishing Company, Inc., New York City.

MARTIN, Paul D. *Arms and Armour.* Charles E. Tuttle Company, Rutland, Vermont.

NICOLLIER, Jean. *Collecting Toy Soldiers.* Charles E. Tuttle Company, Rutland, Vermont.

PETERSON, Harold L. *The Book of the Continental Soldier.* The Stackpole Company, Harrisburg, Pennsylvania.

———— *Arms and Armour in Colonial America, 1526-1783.* The Stackpole Company, Harrisburg, Pennsylvania.

———— *History of Firearms.* The Macmillan Company, New York City.

WILKINSON, Frederick. *Militaria.* Hawthorne Books, Inc., New York City.

MUSICAL INSTRUMENTS & DEVICES

BAINES, Anthony (Ed.). *Musical Instruments through the Ages.* Walker & Company, New York City.

BUCHNER, Alexander. *Mechanical Musical Instruments.* Batchworth Press, London.

EDGERLY, Beatrice. *From the Hunter's Bow. The History and Romance of Musical Instruments.* Edited by Boris Erich Nelson. G. P. Putnam's Sons, New York City.

MOSORIAK, Roy. *The Curious History of Music Boxes.* Lightner Publishing Corporation, Chicago.

ORD-HUME, W. J. G. *Collecting Musical Boxes and How to Repair Them.* Crown Publishers, Inc., New York City.

PAPERWEIGHTS

BERGSTROM, Evangeline H. *Old Glass Paperweights.* Crown Publishers, Inc., New York City.

CLOAK, Evelyn Campbell. *Glass Paperweights of the Bergstrom Art Center.* Crown Publishers, Inc., New York City.

ELVILLE, E. M. *Paperweights and Other Glass Curiosities.* Spring Books, London.

JOKELSON, Paul. *Sulphides. The Art of Cameo Incrustation.* Thomas Nelson & Sons, Camden, New Jersey.

MANHEIM, Frank J. *A Garland of Weights. Some Notes on Collecting French Antique Paperweights for Those Who Don't.* Farrar, Straus & Giroux, New York City.

MELVIN, Jean S. *American Glass Paperweights and Their Makers.* Thomas Nelson & Sons, Camden, New Jersey.

PENNSYLVANIA DUTCH ANTIQUES

ADAMS, Ruth. *Pennsylvania Dutch Art.* World Publishing Company, Cleveland, Ohio.

KAUFFMAN, Henry J. *Pennsylvania Dutch American Folk Art.* Dover Publications, Inc., New York City.

ROBACKER, Earl F. *Pennsylvania Dutch Stuff.* University of Pennsylvania Press, Philadelphia.

———— *Touch of the Dutchland.* A. S. Barnes & Company, Inc., Cranbury, New Jersey.

STOUDT, John Joseph. *Early Pennsylvania Arts and Crafts.* A. S. Barnes & Company, Inc., Cranbury, New Jersey.

TOYS

DAIKEN, Leslie. *Children's Toys Through the Ages.* Spring Books, London.

FOLEY, Daniel J. *Toys Through the Ages.* The Chilton Company, Philadelphia.

FREEMAN, Ruth and Larry. *Yesterday's Toys.* Century House, Watkins Glen, New York.

HERTZ, Louis H. *The Handbook of Old American Toys.* Mark Haber & Company, Wethersfield, Connecticut.

——— *Mechanical Toy Banks.* Mark Haber & Company, Wethersfield, Connecticut.

——— *The Toy Collector.* Funk & Wagnalls, New York City.

APPENDIX

Names and addresses of some of the leading collector periodicals:

Antiques, 551 Fifth Avenue, New York, New York 10017

The Antiques Dealer, 1115 Clifton Avenue, Clifton, New Jersey 07013

The Antiques Journal, P.O. Box 1046, Dubuque, Iowa 52001

Antique Monthly, P.O. Drawer 2, Tuscaloosa, Alabama 35401

Antiques News, Box B, Marietta, Pennsylvania 17547

The Antique Trader, Box 1050, Dubuque, Iowa 52001

Collectors News, 606 Eighth Avenue, Grundy Center, Iowa 50638

Collector's Weekly, Drawer C, 1119, Kermit, Texas 79745

Collector's World, P.O. Box 654, Conroe, Texas 77301

Hobbies, 1006 South Michigan Avenue, Chicago, Illinois 60605

The Mid-America Reporter, Leon, Iowa 50144

National Antiques Review, P.O. Box 619, Portland, Maine 04014

Relics, P.O. Box 3338, Austin, Texas 78764

Spinning Wheel, Exchange Place, Hanover, Pennsylvania 17331

Tri-State Trader, P.O. Box 90, Knightstown, Indiana 46148